Understanding PreK from a Child's Perspective

By: Dr. Angela Sansone

Disclosure

This book is based on my dissertation research that was conducted at a preschool in Trenton, NJ. The names of the school, students, and teachers have been changed to protect confidentiality. Please keep in mind that the preschool students chose their own pseudonyms. I conducted all the interviews and observations, so I can attest to their truthfulness.

This book is a more accessible version of my dissertation. Many of the passages are the same as in the academic book I wrote, *Preschool Teacher-Student Interactions and Expectations* published by LAP Lambert. However, for this book, I wanted to focus more on showing what the classrooms and interactions looked like to the students, so I removed much of the scholarly interpretation that I had placed on the observations and interviews, allowing the children's voices to shine through.

Introduction

Publicly funded preschool programs have come to play an important role in shaping young children's lives in the United States. The enrollment in state funded preschool programs has drastically increased since 2002 to more than 1.3 million four-year-olds as of 2012 (Barnett, Carolan, Fitzgerald, & Squires, 2012). Publicly funded preschool continues to exist in forty of the fifty states and the District of Columbia despite budget cuts in the 2011-2012 school year (Barnett et. al, 2012).

In 1998, New Jersey established the Abbott Preschool Program, in response to Abbott v. Burke (a case from 1985). This program provided free preschool for children aged three and four in thirty-one school districts in New Jersey. The districts chosen to have this program are low-income districts in which the typical cost of preschool is prohibitive to the families. The benefits of this program, besides the free preschool, are as follows:

- Teachers must have a bachelor's degree and a NJ Preschool through Grade Three certification.
- Classes are capped at fifteen students.
- Every class has a teacher assistant.
- All preschools in this program must use one of the research-based curricula chosen by New Jersey.

The education level of the teachers and small class sizes makes providing individual attention much easier. Additionally, having a trained assistant in each classroom ensures better monitoring of the students, so there should be less injuries. Thus, the staff are able to interact more frequently with each child, plan and monitor activities more effectively, and spend the time to really get to know each family.

There has been ongoing research in these 31 districts that has showed the continuous benefits of attendance. Students who attended the Abbott Preschool Program were assessed in kindergarten and first grade. It was found that "one year of the Abbott Preschool Program had an effect size of 0.18 (p<.05) for receptive vocabulary and the two year effect size was 0.38 (p < 01)" (Frede, Jung, Barnett, & Figueras, 2009, p. 17-18).

This leads people to believe that every Abbott preschool is providing effective teaching and assisting the students in preparing for kindergarten and beyond. However, education, training, and curriculum can only equalize so much. Each classroom has its own set of expectations and atmosphere developed by the teaching staff. Unfortunately, most of the research focuses on environmental scores, test scores, teacher interviews, and family interviews to gauge the effectiveness. Most time, the students are not interviewed or even asked for their opinions on their experience.

This book looks at in-depth research conducted in two Abbott Preschool classrooms. Observations were done by the author from January to June 2012. The teachers in each classroom were interviewed three times. The teachers also identified one high achieving student and one low achieving student from their classes. These focal students were interviewed twice.

Background

The School

Hampton Center was purposefully selected as the setting for this study because this is the school in which I was teaching at the time. Hampton is also well suited to the study of teacher expectations and interactions with students that differ racially from themselves because it has a diverse teacher population. Of the seven certified teachers at the school, there are 29 five Caucasian teachers, two African American teachers, and one Hispanic teacher. The student population is much less diverse, primarily consisting of African-American children of lower socio-economic status; of the 105 preschool aged-children, there are two Caucasian students, two Hispanic students, and two Middle-Eastern students. All the students qualify for subsidized lunch, which means that this student population is considered low income.

This preschool operates under the state funded mandates of the Abbott v. Burke, New Jersey Supreme Court case. The basic program standards for each preschool classroom in a former Abbott district is a maximum of fifteen children per classroom, with each classroom having a teacher and a teacher assistant (Frede et. al., 2009). Every teacher has a bachelor's and P-3 certification in the state of New Jersey, and the teacher assistants have or are working towards a Child Development Associate. This is a full day preschool program operating from 7:30 am-5:30 pm. Hampton uses the Creative Curriculum, one of the four curriculum models permitted for state funded preschools in New Jersey (Frede et. al., 2009). Creative Curriculum provided sample schedules, information about time spent in teacher-directed and student-directed activities, lesson plan formats, and trainings for the teachers.

The Teachers

For teachers, I chose to include those who have taught at Hampton Center for more than five years, are Caucasian, have no advanced degrees or specialty training other than their Preschool through grade 3 teaching certification. By choosing participants that have worked as teachers for more than five years I hoped to be able to avoid the focus on classroom management issues that comes from the inexperience of brand-new teachers. Teachers were also chosen based on their educational levels. I chose teachers who had their bachelor's degree in Early Childhood Education, but had no further degrees; this was done in order to ensure that the teachers' reactions to the children were based on their own experience, not the current educational trends. Teacher A, Becky, is Caucasian and has been working at Hampton Center for 8 years. Teacher B, Jane, is also Caucasian and has been working at Hampton Center for 7 years. These teachers have been working in adjoining classrooms for the last three years. Table 1 contains the descriptive data for the teachers.

The Students

A total of four students were selected to participate in this study. Two African American students were purposefully chosen from each classroom using several criteria. First, both students had to be verbally articulate and able to actively participate in interviews. I included a male and a female student from each class in order to ensure that gender was accounted for as a variable. I also had the teachers assist me in the selection to ensure that the two students from each class represented different ends of the academic spectrum; one student from each class was designated as a high achiever by the teacher while the other is considered a lower achiever by the teacher. This difference in achievement allowed me to see the differentiation in expectations based on the teachers' conception of the students' academic abilities.

The two students from classroom B were Princess and Diego, four-year-old African American students. Princess was born in NJ, but her family emigrated from Africa six years ago. Ms. Becky considers Princess to be a smart, motivated student. This was Princess' second year at Hampton Center. Diego's family is from the area surrounding Hampton Center in NJ; his parents went to the local high school. Ms. Becky considered Diego to be one of the slower academic students in her class; this was Diego's second year at Hampton Center.

The two students from classroom B were Dora and Bink, four-year-old African American preschool students. Dora comes from a family who has lived in NJ near Hampton Center for the past ten years. Ms. Jane considered her to be an observant student. This was her second year at Hampton Center, and her old sister and half-brother have both attended Hampton Center as well. Bink was born in Jamaica, but his family moved to New Jersey when he was an infant. Ms. Jane said "Bink is loving, but not one of the quickest academic students." This was his first year at Hampton Center.

PreK A

Ms. Becky is a confident Caucasian teacher of eight years, who teaches a class of fifteen predominately African American children. Ms. Becky's confidence as a teacher was evident from the moment we started talking about this research project. For example, when I mentioned that I was considering including her classroom in this study, Ms. Becky said, "No problem. This would be a great classroom for your project. You always know what you'll get in my class" (conversation, February 20, 2012). Not only does Ms. Becky have confidence in her teaching but so does the community as evidenced by the many requests she receives from parents for their children to be placed in this class. During the 2011-2012 school year, eight out of the fifteen children were placed in PreK A as a result of parent requests.

Purpose of Preschool

Ms. Becky believes that the purpose of preschool is "To prepare them (children) for kindergarten, basically learning letters, numbers, the basics" (interview, April 20, 2012). She told me "my lesson plans provide exactly what children need to prepare for kindergarten" (interview, April 20, 2012).

As Ms. Becky explained to me, "I set my classroom up in interest areas according to Creative Curriculum" (interview, April 20, 2012). Ms. Becky's classroom consists of nine interest areas: toys and games, library and writing, art, discovery, computers, sand and water, blocks, dramatic play, and music and movement. To achieve her academic aims, each of the areas of the classroom is labeled, and all the toys have picture and word labels on the containers and shelves. This labeling provides the opportunity for matching, one-to-one correspondence and prereading skills both when choosing toys and cleaning up. The materials in each area also supplement the academic goals focused on by Ms. Becky. For example, Ms. Becky added menus, books about cooking and families, and calculators to dramatic play to assist the children with pre-reading skills and counting. The block area held toys that assist children with learning letters and mathematical concepts such as alphabet blocks, books on building and architecture, and tape measures. The discovery area held a number of toys for learning about comparisons, such as scales, matching games, and books about different animals and habitats. In addition, there were many items that encouraged learning mathematics such as number puzzles, patterning blocks, parquetry, and nesting blocks. The sand and water tables featured items to help children learn about measurement, such as measuring cups and graduated cylinders. The writing area and library contained supplies that assisted children in learning about letters, writing, and phonetics, such as letter puzzles, letter tracers, rhyming games, and alliteration games. The art area even contained materials to assist the children with academic pursuits, such as books on color mixing, a variety of writing implements, and geometric tracers.

Ms. Becky's academic expectations are also evident in the posters adorning the walls of the classroom; these posters depict the alphabet, numerals 1-20, basic shapes, colors, and the classroom rules. There is a planning board in the whole group area, which also serves as the music area; this planning board not only allows the students to choose their own areas but also provides the spelling of each area and each child's name. There are also displays on the walls made of the children's work. Child-written names and stories graced the walls near the library and writing areas. Student drawings, paintings and collages were displayed at children's eye level near the art table. However, the bulletin boards in the hallway leading up to the classroom were comprised of more teacher-directed work, such as photographs of the children glued to coloring pages with the teacher's writing relaying the children's quote about the season. While

Ms. Becky incorporated a lot of student work into the displays in her classroom, this work

clearly shows her emphasis on academics. For example, a display in the toys and games area is

comprised of children's depictions of counting bears with numerals written by the children under

each bear signifying the total of bears on the page. There were a few pictures of the children

utilizing the classroom equipment, but there were no other displays that reflected the culture or

backgrounds of the children in the classroom.

Whole Group

Ms. Becky's academic goals permeated not only the classroom environment, but also the

activities that she planned. During the four whole group times that I observed, Ms. Becky

concentrated on preliteracy and mathematical skill development by asking "display questions to

which she already knew the answer" (Cazden, 2001, p. 46). In preschool, play is supposed to be

student driven and chosen, allowing each child to learn in their own manner (Copple &

Bredekamp, 2009). She maintained the pretense of playing with the students by providing

cheerful songs and colorful toys and books, but only gave playing with the students lip service as

all observed activities were teacher-directed and provided limited opportunities for children to

express their interests or knowledge. As the following vignette shows, Ms. Becky limited her

whole group time to scripted song choices, developmentally inappropriate repetitious recitations,

and "inauthentic" (Cazden, 2001, p. 46) questions, those that do not allow students to elaborate

or share their knowledge. This can be seen in the following observation from whole group:

> Ms. Becky walks over to the carpet, sits on a chair: "Eyes on me."
>
> Each child sits on his/her individual previously assigned shape

Ms. Becky sings (and signs): "Hello hello hello and how are you? I'm fine I'm fine and I hope that you are too.

All the children sing and sign along.

When the song is over, Ms. Becky: "Calendar helper please come up."

The calendar helper goes to the board.

Ms. Becky: "PreK A, what month is it?"

Children: "April."

Ms. Becky: "Let's count to see what day of the week we're on. Ready calendar helper?" The calendar helper, Bret, points to the numerals on the calendar with a pointer as Ms. Becky assists with the task by directing the child to the correct numerals. Ms. Becky watches as the children say the number that corresponds to the numeral pointed to by the calendar helper.

As the children count, Ms. Becky: "I want to hear my friends counting." She counts with them. Then, Ms. Becky: "So today is the twentieth day of what month?"

Children: "April."

Ms. Becky: "What year is it?"

Children: "2012."

Ms. Becky: "Right, and what season are we in?"

Children: "Spring."

Ms. Becky: "Show me the sign for spring."

The children sign Spring (observation, April 20, 2012).

Morning meetings or circle time have a long history in the early childhood curriculum. Scholars of early childhood education argue that the purpose of bringing children together is to create a community that values and respects the sharing of children's ideas. Similarly, the Creative Curriculum calls for large group time to provide time for children to experience belonging to a group and practicing the rules of this group (Dodge, Heroman, Colker, and Bickart, 2010). Thus, circle time or meeting time is supposed to help children learn academic concepts in a low stakes environment and enable children and teacher to effectively communicate with each other and share ideas. While the teacher controls the discourse to some extent, there is supposed to be opportunities for student input as well.

Activities.

Whole group in Ms. Becky's class was very formulaic and focused, almost exclusively during my observations, on preliteracy and numeracy skills. The format in the opening vignette was followed every day I visited the classroom. For Ms. Becky consistency for these children was key because "children need consistency to learn. Consistency and order helps children understand time concepts, such as now, then, and later" (interview, April, 20, 2012). Given her beliefs, it is not surprising that every whole group I observed consisted of the same format and songs. Similarly, the content taught in small group also did not vary much over the four observations. In the following paragraphs, I will describe how Ms. Becky taught numeracy and preliteracy skills during whole group.

Numeracy was often taught through the use of calendar. According to Etheridge and King (2005), calendar is a common practice in early education that is developmentally appropriate for teaching counting and patterns as long as it is not taught through teacher-directed, whole group instruction. The calendar, in PreK A, consisted of a poster-sized calendar on the wall in the front of the whole group area. The month was on the top of the calendar next to the year, with the day of the week directly to the left of the calendar. The instructional event of calendar involved Ms. Becky using the particular month and day of the year to teach number identification and sequencing. This can be seen in the following observation:

> The calendar helper, Bret, (a student chosen by Ms. Becky) counts
> to 20 with the class, pointing to each printed number on the calendar with
> a pointer as he counts.
>
> Ms. Becky: "I want to hear my friends counting."
>
> She counts with them.
>
> Ms. Becky: "So today is the twentieth day of what month?"
>
> Children: "April" (observation, April 20, 2012).

An almost identical pattern can be seen in the following observation. The second whole group observation:

> The calendar helper, Cece, (a student chosen by Ms. Becky) stands
> and points to each numeral on the calendar with a pointer as she counted
> with the children to 30.
>
> All the children count in rote fashion together: 1, 2, 3, 4, 5,…to 30
> without skipping numbers.
>
> Ms. Becky: "So today's the 30th day of what month?"
>
> Children: "April" (observation, April 30, 2012).

The use of calendar in these observations is almost identical. The only difference is the amount of numbers counted. Every day, the children were expected to count to the day of the month as a way to get them to connect the written numeral to the number that children orally counted.

Numeracy was also taught in large group by counting children's yes/no responses to the question of the day. Ms. Becky also concluded each whole group with counting usually by having the children compare the amounts of children who answered yes and no to the question of the day; this comparison was based on the pictures of each child that Ms. Becky placed on the question of the day board under the answer each child gave. This can be seen in the following excerpt from an observation:

Ms. Becky: "Let's count how many friends said that they have been to the zoo?"

The children count with Ms. Becky as she points to each picture with her finger, "One, two, three, four, five, six, seven, eight."

Ms. Becky: "Let's count how many friends said that they have not been to the zoo?"

The children count with Ms. Becky, "One, two, three, four, five, six."

Ms. Becky: "Eight is bigger than six."

Children: "Eight is bigger than six."

Ms. Becky: "Six is smaller than eight."

Children: "Six is smaller than eight."

Ms. Becky and the children: "Our conclusion is more of us said that we have been to the zoo" (observation, May 17, 2012).

Similarly, in the second observation, the children also counted and compared the results of the question of the day, in which thirteen children answered yes to the question "Did you have fun at home?" and zero children said no. Each child had placed a picture of himself or herself under the answer of either yes or no.

Ms. Becky: "Count how many friends had fun at home."

Children: "1, 2, 3, 4, 5, 6, 7, 8, 9, 10, 11, 12, 13."

Ms. Becky: "Thirteen of us said that we had fun at home. Let's count how many of us said that we did not have fun at home."

Children: "Zero."

Ms. Becky: "Right. Which number is bigger?"

Children: "Thirteen" (observation, April 30, 2012).

By totaling up children's responses to a question in this way, Ms. Becky used counting to teach comparisons of quantities.

Preliteracy skills include letter identification, phonological awareness, print awareness, narrative skills, and vocabulary (Dodge et. al., 2012). These preliteracy skills were taught primarily through the spelling of the month, day and season, a morning message, and a closed-ended question that were asked each day during whole group. Ms. Becky also wrote a morning message on the board and pointed out the punctuation and capitalization when introducing the message to the class as can be seen in the following observation:

Ms. Becky: "PreK A, what month is it?"

Children: "April."

Ms. Becky: "Let's count to see what day of the week we're on. Ready calendar helper?"

Then, the calendar helper, Bret, uses a pointer to indicate each numeral as the class counts to 20.

Ms. Becky: "I want to hear my friends counting." She counts with them.

Ms. Becky: "So today is the twentieth day of what month?"

Children: "April."

Ms. Becky: "What year is it?"

Children: "2012."

Ms. Becky: "Right, and what season are we in?"

Children: "Spring."

Ms. Becky: "Show me the sign for spring."

The children sign Spring.

Ms. Becky: "Good." Then, she sings Days of the Week, with the children singing and clapping along. Next, they sing, "Do you know what day it is?"

Ms. Becky: "What letter does today start with?"

Children: "F."

Ms. Becky: "What sound does F make?"

Children: "Fffff" (The children make an F sound).

Ms. Becky: "Today is Friday."

Children: "Today is Friday."

Then, Ms. Becky: "Let's do our months."

Ms. Becky and the children sing the months of the year.

Ms. Becky and the children: "Today is Friday, April 20, 2012."

Ms. Becky: "Thank you."

Then, she and the children sing, "What's the weather?" When the song is over, Ms. Becky: "Show me PreK A?"

The children make the sign for sunny.

The weather watcher then tells the class the weather report. He points to and reads a sentence that states: "Today's weather is hot and sunny."

Children: "Today's weather is hot and sunny."

Ms. Becky: "Now, it's time for the morning message. Ms. Becky will read it first, then I will ask you to read it."

Ms. Becky had written the morning message on the whiteboard before the children sat for whole group. Then, she reads while pointing at the words with her finger, "Good morning boys and girls. Today is Friday, April 20, 2012. We are going to watch a movie today."

Next, Ms. Becky asks the girls to say the message. All the girls stand up: "Good morning boys and girls. Today is Friday, April 20, 2012. We are going to watch a movie today." Then, they sit down.

Then, she calls on the boys to say the message. All the boys stand up: "Good morning boys and girls. Today is Friday, April 20, 2012. We are going to watch a movie today." Then, they sit down.

All: "Good morning boys and girls. Today is Friday, April 20, 2012. We are going to watch a movie today."

Ms. Becky: "It's time for the question of the day. I want to know,

Did you have fun at the soccer clinic?" she asks each child individually.

They sign yes and spell yes; then Ms. Becky puts their picture under Yes

on the question of the day board (observation, April, 20, 2012).

Looking across the four observations of whole group, the pattern did not vary. In terms of numeracy, there was always counting and comparison of quantities. In terms of preliteracy, there was spelling, in which the message was written on the board by Ms. Becky prior to the children attending whole group. According to DAP, adult-directed forced repetition exhausts and frustrates children (Gestwicki, 2011); however, Ms. Becky seemed to find this repetition to be an integral part of her class' whole group as it occurred during each of the four whole group observations that I observed. This practice suggests that Ms. Becky does not have high expectations of her students. She seemed to assume that her students needed a lot of repetition to be able to learn the concepts she taught during whole group. The whole group times were also very long, lasting up to forty minutes, which is a very long time to except four-year-olds to sit with their legs folded, paying attention. I had trouble, as an observer, focusing for that long on this repetitive experience.

Whole group talk.

Oral language opportunities during whole group provide opportunities for children to share their ideas, thoughts and emotions creating a classroom community. Whole group in PreK A, however, provided little to no chance for the children to express their own ideas. Ms. Becky tended to dominate talking time during whole group and when choosing questions to ask during whole group, Ms. Becky tended to choose "display" or "inauthentic" (Cazden, 2001) questions so that there was little opportunity for children to elaborate on their answers, share their knowledge, or connect with others who had similar answers. According to Cazden (2001), these types of questions simply test student information retention or co-opt students into participation without any genuine interest in the knowledge that the students have.

In the four observations of whole group, Ms. Becky asked twenty-two "display" (Cazden, 2001) questions and three "inauthentic" (Cazden, 2001) questions, which did not allow for elaboration. A "display" question occurs when a teacher poses a question to the class in the guise of eliciting participation, but the teacher knows the answer to the question before asking. An example of a "display" question asked by Ms. Becky is "What month is it?" which Ms. Becky asked every day in large group. Whereas the questions of the day that Ms. Becky asked such as, "Did you have fun at the soccer clinic?" (observation, April 20, 2012) or "Have you ever been to the zoo?" (observation, May 17, 2012) are examples of the "inauthentic" questions. These kinds of questions are "inauthentic" because Ms. Becky is simply co-opting students to participate in order to break up what could be seen as a lecture. Her intent is to seem like she is giving the children a chance to share their experiences without allowing for actual communication to take place. Ms. Becky is reluctant to relinquish any control of whole group to her students; suggesting that she does think that they have knowledge that is important enough to be shared. This is, unfortunately, preparing Ms. Becky's students for the reality of many classrooms in which low-income, Black students are not seen as having any knowledge worth contributing to classroom conversations.

Over the four group observations, I only saw Ms. Becky ask one potentially open-ended question, which could have elicited information about children's experiences and helped them to make connections between out of and in-school experiences:

Ms. Becky: "It's time for the question of the day. Today's question is, Did you have fun at home?" Ms. Becky takes a picture of each child out of a small box, choosing at random. When she says the child's name, she gives them time to answer what they did that was fun at home.

A girl: "I ate some pretzels and I had some fun under the covers on my bed."

A boy: "Uh, I play with my brother."

After each child's response, Ms. Becky: "That sounds like fun. Thank you for sharing."

When all the children have had a turn, Ms. Becky: "Count how many friends had fun at home."

Children: "1, 2, 3, 4, 5, 6, 7, 8, 9, 10, 11, 12, 13."

Ms. Becky: "Thirteen of us said that we had fun at home. Let's count how many of us said that we did not have fun at home."

Children: "Zero."

Ms. Becky: "Right. Which number is bigger?"

Children: "Thirteen."

Ms. Becky: "Thirteen is a bigger number than 0 and 0 is a smaller number. What is our conclusion?"

Children: "All of us said that we had fun at home" (observation, April 30, 2012).

While Ms. Becky seemed to ask about the children's experiences through the question: Did you have fun at home?, Ms. Becky did not ask any follow up questions or point out anything about the children's answers; she simply moved on to her planned math lesson. Another example of how a possibly open-ended question was closed by Ms. Becky occurred on May 17, 2012 when the question of the day was: Have you ever been to the zoo?.

Ms. Becky: "It's time for the question of the day. Today's question is, have you ever been to the zoo?" Ms. Becky takes a picture of each child out of a small box, choosing at random. When she says the child's name, she did not give the children time to elaborate about their zoo experience:

A boy: "Y E S, yes."

A girl: "N O, no."

When all the children have answered, Ms. Becky: "Let's count how many friends said that they have been to the zoo?"

Children and Ms. Becky: "One, two, three, four, five, six, seven, eight."

Ms. Becky: "Let's count how many friends said that they have not been to the zoo?"

Children and Ms. Becky: "One, two, three, four, five, six."

Ms. Becky: "Eight is bigger than six."

Children: "Eight is bigger than six."

Ms. Becky: "Six is smaller than eight."

Children: "Six is smaller than eight."

Children and Ms. Becky: "Our conclusion is more of us said that we have been to the zoo" (observation, May 17, 2012).

As can be seen in this observation, once again the opportunity for children to describe their experiences at the zoo, if they have been to the zoo, or to share knowledge of animals is foregone for Ms. Becky's script. Ms. Becky uses "inauthentic" questions to feign interest in the children's experiences, but only uses these questions to further her preliteracy goals.

Each occurrence of whole group time that I observed Pre-K A followed the same teacher-directed pattern: This whole group routine supported Ms. Becky's academic goals through strict adherence to the routine of call to the carpet, calendar, weather, morning message and question of the day. The same songs were also used in whole group during the routines: hello song, days of the week, months of the year, and what's the weather. During an informal conversation, Ms. Becky said, "I always use the same songs. I like it better that way" (conversation, June 14, 2012). The only change in routine occurred on June 13, 2012. While Ms. Becky followed the same predictable pattern for whole group time: calendar, weather, morning message, this whole group deviated from the others I observed because Ms. Becky substituted graduation songs for the question of the day. Since this observation happened at the end of the school year, Ms. Becky focused on the upcoming graduation, by rehearsing songs that she had chosen and had been using for a number of years.

By controlling the interactions, song choices, and questions, Ms. Becky controlled the whole group experience. The strict adherence to her own whole group time script allowed Ms. Becky to maintain control over interactions within the large group of children. By not allowing the children to give explanations about their experiences, Ms. Becky stifled her students' opportunity for social-emotional growth or individuality. Preschoolers need opportunities to express themselves and their opinions; these opportunities allow preschoolers to engage in the process of identification, finding out about their own identities and their place in the society. In order for children to engage in this process, they need to be allowed time to work on their social interactions and express their ideas as active listeners (Gestwicki, 2011). However, by maintaining control over the talk and content of large group, Ms. Becky focused on her academic expectations of preliteracy and numeracy to the detriment of possibly enhancing the children's social-emotional growth.

From a developmental perspective, this use of whole group may be seen as inappropriate, but utilizing large group in this way might also be seen as an attempt by Ms. Becky to teach children of color "content that other families from a different cultural orientation provide at home" (Delpit, 2006, p. 30), which is to say that Ms. Becky is providing her students with the knowledge of how to succeed in a white, middle-class society. She speaks in authoritative tones and provides the academic knowledge that should assist the children in kindergarten preparation. According to Delpit, child centered curricula reflects a set of middle-class values, she says that African American students do not learn this way. This is not to say that Ms. Becky should be only providing basic skills teaching in her class; however, some scholars would agree Ms. Becky is teaching her students the behaviors and rhetoric that is expected of children to be successful in school (Delpit, 2006).

Small Group

In Creative Curriculum, small group time is used by teachers to introduce new concepts, teach skills, encourage conversation, and focus on observing specific children (Dodge et. al., 2012). According to Ms. Becky the purpose of small group is readying children for school. In her words, she uses small group time to "learn and practice skills for kindergarten" (interview, April 20, 2012).

Small group in PreK A, like whole group, is controlled by Ms. Becky. She chooses the activity and the group. For example, during my observations, I did not see Ms. Becky consult the children for ideas to add to her lessons. Small groups ranged in size from one child to four children in PreK A although Ms. Becky had the same two children in small group together each time I observed. This can be seen in Table 1 Ms. Becky centered her small group lessons on math and literacy.

Table 1 – Small Group Observation Focuses for PreK A

Date	Theme	Focus	Activity
4/24/12	Butterflies	Shapes	Butterfly shape sorters
5/10/12	Butterflies	Counting backwards	Storybook read aloud *Ten Wriggly, Wiggly Caterpillars* by Debbie Tarbett Children counted along with story.
5/24/12	Zoo	Patterns	Storybook read aloud *Lots and Lots of Zebra Stripes* by Stephen R. Swinburne Children identified the patterns in the book.
6/6/12	Father's Day	Reading comprehension	Storybook read aloud *What Daddies Can't Do* By Douglas Wood Children answered questions asked by Ms. Becky that referenced the story.

To enact small groups, Ms. Becky chose one or two of the learning objectives from Creative Curriculum linking the objective of the lesson to the theme being investigated by the class and crafting an activity that would show her the children's knowledge as it pertained to those objectives. Regardless of the theme, the small group activities chosen by Ms. Becky always linked to math or literacy. When the children were studying butterflies, Ms. Becky used the butterfly sorting game to teach about shapes and a counting book about caterpillars to emphasize numeracy. When the theme was zoo, Ms. Becky used a book about animal prints to teach about patterns, and when the theme was Father's Day, she used a book about fathers to assist the children in learning reading comprehension skills. The books that Ms. Becky chose for these small group lessons were written by Caucasian authors, and while they related to the themes of the week, these books were not necessarily relevant to the children's experiences, especially the ones about fathers since many of the students did not have fathers who interacted with them frequently.

At the beginning of each small group, which occurred in the late morning following whole group and before outdoor play, Ms. Becky introduced the lesson. Ms. Becky told the students in her small group which objectives they would be focusing on and showed them the materials. She then went into the activity as the following excerpt illustrates:

> Ms. Becky brings over the Shape Butterflies Game to the table in the toys and games area where a child is sitting alone. She opens the container: "I want you to look at the shapes and tell me what they are. What shape is that?"
>
> Child: "Circle."
>
> Ms. Becky: "Can you tell me about the circle?"
>
> Child: "The circle is kind of like a ball."
>
> Ms. Becky: "A circle is kind of like a ball." She repeated as she took notes. Then, she holds up a star. "What shape is this?"
>
> Child: "A star."
>
> Ms. Becky: "Can you tell me about a star?"

Child: "A star be up the sky."

She repeats the phrase as she takes notes. Ms. Becky: "Now you can use these shapes and match them to make butterflies." She puts all the pieces on the table in front of the child. "Find the matching wings. You can build your own butterflies" (observation, April 20, 2012).

This small group stuck out when compared with the other three small group observations from Pre K A as it was the only small group activity that used a toy instead of books as the main teaching material. However, as the above vignette shows Ms. Becky's academic goals were present in her small group activities as they were in whole group. Ms. Becky's purpose for the above activity was shape recognition and description. During this small group activity, Ms. Becky asked "display" questions, focusing on repetitions of shape names, shape descriptions, and counting, similar to the information that she elicited with her questions during whole group.

In this more typical observation, Ms. Becky read a book, written by a white author, to the children, and asked them "display" questions that focused on their recall of previously taught knowledge about the structure of books:

Two children sit at a table with Ms. Becky.

Ms. Becky held up a book: "The title of this book is What Dad's Can't Do. We're going to read this story about dads." She read the author's name: "What does the author do?"

First child: "Wrote the book."

Ms. Becky reads the illustrator's name: "What does the illustrator do?"

Second child: "Draw all the pictures."

Ms. Becky turns to the title page: "What is this page called?"

First child: "Title page."

Ms. Becky: "On this page we have?"

Both children: "The title, the author, the illustrator and the publisher"

(observation, June 6, 2012).

Ms. Becky adopted the role of tester when she asked questions to assess the children's knowledge retention from previous lessons, as seen in the above vignette. This was also indicated on her lesson plan on May 24, 2012. Ms. Becky showed the children the title page of the *Lots and Lots of Zebra Stripes* and asked, Do you remember what page this is? to follow up on the lesson she taught about parts of a book the previous day during story time.

During small groups, Ms. Becky seemed to take on the role of observer, but her observations were merely tests of the children's knowledge. In each small group Ms. Becky took notes as the children used the materials or interacted with the story book; this note taking seemed to follow the developmentally appropriate role of teacher as observer (Gestwicki, 2011). However, Ms. Becky did not use these observations to adapt her lessons to the children's needs; she used her notes as a checklist to show what the children learned.

While Ms. Becky took observation notes during each small group, she did not seem to use her observations of individual children as a tool to plan for the next small group activity. During the second interview, Ms. Becky stated, "Diego likes the bikes and the balls. He really likes the balls outside" (interview, May 16, 2012), but during the eight weeks of observations in PreK A, Ms. Becky did not incorporate these interests into the studies/themes. Ms. Becky asserted her power by using the topics to study as a way of maintaining her privilege as teacher and exercising her authority as to what warrants attention (Faubion, 1994, p. 344). In addition to maintaining power and authority by choosing the topics for learning, Ms. Becky also chose to approach her academic lessons based on her understanding of what children should learn, not based on her observations of the children she teaches. This assertion of power by authority figures prepared Ms. Becky's students for future encounters with white authority figures, especially educators, who will feel that they have the expertise and therefore must have all the power over their low-income, Black students.

DAP and Ms. Becky

The academic discourse espoused by Ms. Becky is in contrast to the developmental discourse that frames best practices in early childhood. Developmentally Appropriate Practice, (DAP) is an approach to teaching using best practices, as agreed upon by a consensus of early childhood professionals and endorsed by NAEYC (National Association for Educators of Young Children). According to DAP, academics in preschool should be taught through play (Copple & Bredekamp, 2009; Gestwicki, 2011). Ms. Becky claims to teach through play, however her focus on academics over the children's other developmental needs skews how she allows play to occur within her classroom. Play in PreK A is not initiated by children's interests or allowed to progress according to the children's desire, instead play is used as a means to teach academic concepts through toys and activities chosen and controlled by Ms. Becky. According to DAP, academics integrated into teaching with play can be appropriate for preschool aged children, however, "when what you have is a narrowly defined set of specific facts and skills being taught apart from meaningful context and without attention to engaging children's interest, such a distorted form of academic leaning is clearly not appropriate for young children" (Copple & Bredekamp, 2009, p. 329).

Ms. Becky's Interactions and Expectations of Focal Children

Ms. Becky's academic goals also translated into her interactions with the two focal children --Princess and Diego -- and her expectations of them. While both children had similar backgrounds and were of the same age group, they had different expectations placed on them. In this section, I will first discuss Princess and then will discuss Diego's experiences in the classroom.

Princess.

Princess is a young four. There are a number of children in PreK A who were five by November and December, but Princess would not be five until the end of July. Princess conformed to Ms. Becky's academic goals, and as a consequence Princess received a lot of praise and was seen by Ms. Becky as a good student. In an informal conversation on April 22, Ms. Becky said, "Princess is a wonderful student to have in class. She always listens."

As part of the Creative Curriculum, family conference forms are provided four times a year. When looking at the parent conference forms for Princess, Ms. Becky's belief in Princess' academic abilities is clear. Ms. Becky described Princess's cognitive strengths on the Spring Family Conference Form as being able to identify all twenty-six upper case and lower-case letters, identifying numerals up to twenty, counting up to thirty-nine, identifying all colors and shapes, as well as writing and identifying her full name. Also, on the spring conference forms, Ms. Becky set goals for each child for the last semester (April 17, 2012). For Princess, Ms. Becky's goals were "Initiate, join in, and sustain positive interactions with a small group of two to three children. Match beginning sounds of some words" (April 17, 2012). When asked to describe Princess, Ms. Becky said,

> Princess has been really shy. She's been coming out of her shell a
> little bit. She voices her needs and opinions. She'll talk back to her friends
> now. Well, not really talk back but respond. If they do something that she
> doesn't like, she'll tell them. She's made new friendships now. She has a few

friends that she likes to play with. She's very, very bright, but she kind of

lacks a little social (interview, May 16, 2012).

However, while she spoke of Princess' social needs during an interview and on her family

conference form, Ms. Becky did not include any social development goals on her lesson plans. Ms.

Becky did not state how she would help Princess develop social skills nor did I see any indication of

the teaching of social development during the eight observations.

Ms. Becky focused on Princess' academic adeptness and saw Princess as a student who

listens and follows directions. Therefore, Princess received much praise and little redirection in the

classroom. During the four whole group observations, Princess was praised three times and never

redirected. Similarly, during the four small group times, Princess was praised fifteen times and never

redirected. Princess also never seemed to be ignored during activities with Ms. Becky because

Princess readily answered Ms. Becky's questions and in a way that validated Ms. Becky's academic

goals. For example, during the small group on April 24, 2012, Ms. Becky encouraged Princess as she

worked with the butterfly shapes:

> Ms. Becky held up a triangle: "What shape is this?"
>
> Princess: "A triangle. It has three points and three sides."
>
> Ms. Becky: "Good."

Ms. Becky also provided encouragement and an opportunity for Princess to express herself during

the small group observation on May 24, 2012:

> Ms. Becky: "This book is a little different. Instead of an illustrator,
>
> there's a photographer. Do you know what a photographer does?"
>
> Princess: "Take pictures."
>
> Ms. Becky: "Right, so all the pictures in this book are not drawings.
>
> They're pictures."

By answering questions in the way Ms. Becky expected, Princess conforms to Ms. Becky's view of the ideal student. This could also be seen during whole group.

Ms. Becky used Princess as a model of appropriate behavior during whole group. When Ms. Becky asked the children to gather for whole group on April 30, 2012, Princess was one of the first to sit on the carpet. Ms. Becky said, loudly enough for the entire class to hear, "I love how Princess is sitting." Ms. Becky also smiled at Princess during whole group when Princess was engaging in the expected appropriate behaviors, such as when Princess correctly pointed to each numeral on the calendar when counting during her role as the calendar helper on April 30, 2012. When Princess sat quietly while other children talked during the beginning of whole group on May 17, 2012, Ms. Becky smiled at Princess. These words of approval and smiles encouraged Princess to continue to meet Ms. Becky's expectations and validated Princess' actions.

Princess fit Ms. Becky's prototype of the ideal student. As Graue (2005) showed, the ideal student is the student that the teacher sees as typical and has in mind when designing lessons. For Ms. Becky, the ideal student is a rule follower with high level self-regulation skills. This student is quiet, responding to questions with a raised hand and correct answer when called on. Ms. Becky's ideal student is excelling in developing literacy and numeracy. It is for this ideal student that Ms. Becky has planned her lessons.

Diego.

Diego is a four-year-old, turning five in March. He enjoys physical activity and social interactions, especially playing outside with his friends. He typically shows up for school in jeans, sneakers, and a white T-shirt. In contrast to Princess, Diego, did not conform to Ms. Becky's academic goals or her prototype of a "good" student. Ms. Becky viewed Diego as a lower achiever and tended to focus on his lack of attention. Ms. Becky described Diego in this way, "Diego becomes distracted easily. We need to redirect him often, especially in large group" (interview, May 16, 2012).

Ms. Becky's perception that Diego lacked self-regulation skills was evident in the amount of redirection she engaged in with him. Across the four whole group observations, Diego was redirected five times, in comparison to his fourteen classmates, who were not redirected more than once across the four observations, while he only received praise from Ms. Becky two times during the four whole group observations. During whole group on April 20, 2012, Diego said the morning message while it was the girls' turn to repeat. Ms. Becky said, "Excuse me. While the girls are saying the morning message, the boys need to be quiet. When the boys go, the girls will be quiet." During the question of the day on April 30, 2012, Diego laughed when Princess stuttered while answering the question. Ms. Becky said, "Please stop." By the end of that whole group time (the thirty minutes they had been sitting), Diego began wiggling in his seat; Ms. Becky shook her head and sighed at him. The only times that Diego received praise during whole group was when he repeated what the other children were saying or sat, looking quietly at Ms. Becky.

During the four small group observations, Diego was redirected five times, ignored nine times, and praised five times. During the first small group observation, when the goal of the lesson was to build butterflies by matching the shape on the body to the outline of the shape on the wings. Ms. Becky only praised Diego when he accomplished the academic goal of matching the shapes with the outlines on the butterfly wings. When Diego became confused or hesitated, Ms. Becky redirected his attention back to the shapes instead of focusing on the connections that Diego was making, invalidating his way of approaching the problem:

> Ms. Becky: "Find the matching wings. You can build your own butterflies."

> Diego holds the wings and puts the color that matched next to the body of the same color. The shapes do not fit together.

Ms. Becky: "I like the way you are matching the colors. Look the bodies and the wings have the shapes on them. Can you see that? The bodies and the wings have the shape on them."

Diego puts the heart body and the heart wing together.

Ms. Becky: "Good, you matched the hearts."

Diego tries another shape.

Ms. Becky: "What shape are you matching now?"

Diego: "Blue."

Ms. Becky: "Blue, that's the color. What shape are you matching?"

Diego: "Star."

Ms. Becky: "You found the two stars and matched them together."

Diego tries to make another match.

Ms. Becky: "Ok, let's do that one and play some more later. Just finish your star" (April 24, 2012).

In the above vignette, Ms. Becky provided more praise when Diego was able to complete the match that Ms. Becky expected, and she did not focus on Diego's ability to match colors as a positive outcome because that was not the assigned task.

Similarly, during small group on May 24, 2012, Ms. Becky's goal for the lesson was for the children to display their knowledge about books and then look for patterns based on the photographs in the book. Diego attempted to make his own connections during this lesson:

Ms. Becky holds up a book: "The title of this book is *Lots and Lots of Zebra Stripes*. We're going to read this book about patterns. Then, we're going to look for patterns in the classroom." She reads the author's name and then turns to the title page. "Do you remember what this page is?"

Diego: "Ms. Becky. I have this book."

The other child: "Title page."

Diego: "Ms. Becky. Ms. Becky."

Ms. Becky does not respond. Ms. Becky: "On this page we have?"

The other child and Diego: "The title, the author, the illustrator and

the publisher."

Ms. Becky: "This book is a little different. Instead of an illustrator,

there's a photographer. Do you know what a photographer does?"

Diego: "Can I tell you something?"

Ms. Becky: "Do you know what a photographer does?"

Diego: "Can I tell you something?"

The other child: "Take pictures."

Ms. Becky: "Right, so all the pictures in this book are not drawings.

They're pictures. Yes, Diego, what would you like to say?"

Diego: "I got…I got Elmo book."

Ms. Becky: "Ok."

Diego: "But my dog ripped it up."

Ms. Becky: "Oh ok. I'm sorry to hear that." She continues to talk

about the author and photographer. Then, she reads the book without

interruption. She points out the patterns in the photographs (observation, May

24, 2012).

Ms. Becky's focus on her lesson during this small group causes her to miss an opportunity to

engage Diego in the lesson. Diego found a connection to this book with the book he had at home, but

Ms. Becky dismissed Diego's attempts to engage in conversation about his connection. This

discourages Diego from sharing his interpretations and connections with Ms. Becky. Making this

kind of text-to-text connection is important because connecting learning to children's experiences makes learning more meaningful to the children and aids in remembering concepts (Copple &

Bredekamp, 2009). Because Ms. Becky positioned herself in the academic discourse, which defines

success as correct answers, Diego was seen as less capable by Ms. Becky because he was not able to

answer her questions precisely.

Ms. Becky viewed Diego as a slow learner. In an informal conversation, Ms. Becky said,

"Diego's just not very smart. He doesn't seem to get it, but it's like that sometimes with these

children" (conversation, February 20, 2012); implying that African-American children from low-

income families should not be expected to excel in school. While Ms. Becky only used the phrase

"these children" twice while speaking to me, this phrase is a deficit model reference to "at risk"

students or black students (Delpit, 2006). By placing Diego with the group "these children," Ms.

Becky did not expect Diego to succeed.

Not surprisingly, all of her documentation about Diego focused mostly on his academic

deficits and not on his strengths. On Diego's conference form, Ms. Becky's goals were "Produce the

correct sounds for 10-20 letters. Begin to identify numerals to 10 by name and connect each to

counted objects" (April 17, 2012). Similarly, Ms. Becky's lesson plans for the week of April 23,

2012 included the following individualizations, "Diego needs to work on remembering the names of

shapes; focus on those." Ms. Becky's lesson plans for the week of May 7 stated, "Diego needs help

to stay on task, especially during read alouds." There were only two strengths written on Diego's

conference form, "Diego places objects in two or more groups based on differences in a single

characteristic. Diego fills in the missing rhyming word, generates rhyming words spontaneously."

This complete focus on academic development dismisses other areas in which Diego may have been

succeeding, such as physical development due to his interest in riding bikes and playing ball. Ms.

Becky did not modify her expectations to meet Diego's needs or to complement the areas in which he

showed an interest (Copple & Bredekamp, 2009). In this way, Ms. Becky ignored the "cultural

capital," the social and cultural knowledge that Diego brought to the classroom because it does not match her expectations of what a child needs to learn (Delpit, 2006). As a consequence, Diego was seen as less capable of learning or succeeding.

Unfortunately, Diego is learning that authority figures may not have high opinions of low-income, Black males. He is becoming aware that he is not expected to succeed at school. Ms. Becky's expectations have not helped him gain confidence in his academic or social abilities in preschool.

Similarities and Differences in Ms. Becky's Interactions with Princess and Diego

In PreK A, Princess and Diego seemed to understand the expectations placed on them by Ms. Becky. When asked, "Do you always agree with your teacher?," Diego said, "I always do everything she tells me to do." Princess said, "When we agree, that's very good. When I agree, I say okay. When I do not agree I say no." I asked, "What happens?" Princess said, "I start doing what Ms. Becky do" (interviews, June 13, 2012). These answers show that both Princess and Diego understand that Ms. Becky has the power in the classroom and that disagreeing with her is not a valid choice.

When looking across the observations of Princess and Diego's interactions with Ms. Becky, I noticed that Ms. Becky did have different interactions with Princess and Diego. When Princess and Diego were behaving similarly, that is acting like Ms. Becky's ideal student, both children received equal amounts of praise. In the four whole group times, when Princess and Diego were responding with the same answers, the children both received smiles, such as when they walked over and sat down when Ms. Becky asked on June 13 (observation, June 13, 2012). The interactions Ms. Becky had with both children were similar when both children were perceived to be on task and giving correct answers to her questions, as is shown in the small group observation from May 10, 2012:

Ms. Becky asks Princess and Diego to join her for small group. She

has the book, 10 Wriggly, Wiggly Caterpillars and a box of toy caterpillars.

Ms. Becky reads the book to Princess and Diego, showing them the pictures.

"Ten wriggly, wiggly caterpillars by Debbie Tarbett. Ten crunching caterpillars in the bright sunshine. One fell asleep so then there was. How many were left?"

Princess: "Nine."

Ms. Becky: "Good, Princess."

Ms. Becky: "Nine speedy caterpillars thought they might be late. One was too slow, so that left?"

Princess: "Eight."

Diego looks at the book.

Ms. Becky: "Eight, good. Eight munching caterpillars all in crunching heaven. One got a tummy ache, so that left?"

Princess: "Seven."

Ms. Becky: "Seven, right there. Seven clever caterpillars creeping through some sticks. One got stuck, so that left?"

Diego continues to look at the book.

Princess: "Number six."

Ms. Becky: "Good, Princess, that's the number six. Six singing caterpillars glad to be alive. One stayed to sing, so that left?"

Diego and Princess: "Five."

Ms. Becky: "Good, Diego, five. Five brave caterpillars going to explore. One got lost, so that left?"

Diego and Princess: "Four."

Ms. Becky; "Four daring caterpillars inching up a tree. One fell off, so that left?"

Diego and Princess: "Three."

Ms. Becky: "Right, that's the numeral three. Three cool caterpillars splashing in the dew. One got soaked, so that left?"

Diego and Princess: "Two."

Ms. Becky: "Two, right, that's the numeral two. Two happy caterpillars having so much fun. One got tired, so that left?"

Diego and Princess: "One."

However, when Diego was unable to answer questions posed by Ms. Becky or provided an incorrect response, Ms. Becky was quick to give praise to Princess while either ignoring or directing Diego to pay attention as shown in the small group observation from May 24, 2012:

Ms. Becky is sitting at the table in the discovery, science area with Diego on the left side of her and Princess on the right. Ms. Becky holds up a book: "The title of this book is *Lots and Lots of Zebra Stripes*. We're going to read this book about patterns. Then, we're going to look for patterns in the classroom." She reads the author's name and then turns to the title page. "Do you remember what this page is?"

Diego: "Ms. Becky. I have this book."

Princess: "Title page."

Diego: "Ms. Becky. Ms. Becky."

Ms. Becky does not respond.

Ms. Becky: "On this page we have?"

Princess and Diego: "The title, the author, the illustrator and the publisher."

Ms. Becky: "This book is a little different. Instead of an illustrator, there's a photographer. Do you know what a photographer does?"

Diego: "Can I tell you something?"

Ms. Becky: "Do you know what a photographer does?"

Princess: "Um."

Diego: "Can I tell you something?"

Princess: "Take pictures."

Ms. Becky: "Right, so all the pictures in this book are not

drawings. They're pictures. Yes, Diego, what would you like to say?"

Diego: "I got…I got Elmo book."

Ms. Becky: "Ok."

Diego: "But my dog ripped it up."

Ms. Becky: "Oh ok. I'm sorry to hear that." She continues to talk

about the author and photographer. Then, she reads the book without

interruption. She points out the patterns in the photographs.

During this interaction, Ms. Becky focused on the information that she was looking for.

She ignored Diego's comments about the connection he felt to a book he had at home. Instead,

Becky focused on what she saw as correct answers, which allowed for a comparison of Princess

and Diego. Ms. Becky's actions positioned Princess as the superior student, while relegating

Diego to the position of inferior student.

Both Princess and Diego understood Ms. Becky's perceptions of them. Princess stated,

"Every time she sees me doing good stuff, she says that I'm participating" (interview, May 23,

2012). When asked what she thinks of her teacher, four-year-old Princess said, "Always tells us

to do something. I like her because she has long hair, and I wish I had long hair" (interview, May

23, 2012). However, Diego did not receive the same message from Ms. Becky, stating "She doesn't like me. Teachers don't like boys" (interview, May 23, 2012). While Diego may not realize the reason, he noticed that Ms. Becky treated him differently than Princess and the girls in the classroom.

Summary

> During whole group time children are expected to listen attentively
> and, when appropriate, to converge with 'correct' responses to the
> teacher's questions. The head teacher believes that group time is
> the time when children learn (Lubeck, 1985, p. 74).

This is a description of whole group written by Lubeck as she witnessed it in a Head Start classroom in 1985. For Lubeck, the teacher in the Head Start classroom, like Ms. Becky, was helping to prepare their students to attend school where the curriculum is based on white, middle-class norms. In this way, the expectations of increased self-regulation and correct answers to questions were intended to make the transition to public school easier for the students. PreK A could be seen as a reproduction of this type of whole group in which children attend school to learn the correct answers, provided by the teacher.

As a white woman, Ms. Becky placed a class bias on her students, treating them as though they must be taught in a group and can only be seen to be learning when they are able to repeat the information that was given to them. In this way, Ms. Becky promoted group growth and obedience. By asking mostly closed-ended questions, Ms. Becky did not allow these African American children to learn through 'involvement' style, in which people are able to fluidly build on the ideas of others without waiting turns (Hallum, 2006). Ms. Becky ignores the "cultural capital" that her students could be bringing to the class and eliminates the possibility for social and emotional growth by denying her students the chance to have input into the curriculum (Delpit, 1995; Copple & Bredekamp, 2009). In addition to controlling the discourse in the classroom, Ms. Becky also asserts her power by denying the students representation within the curriculum choosing mostly Euro-centric images as decoration. This is a form of demonstrating institutional power by choosing what knowledge and culture is relevant despite attempts from the students to bring in their own knowledge and personal connections (Copple & Bredekamp, 2009). This type of deficit discourse, of only the teacher having knowledge and being the dominant culture represented in the classroom, is not developmentally appropriate (Copple & Bredekamp, 2009) and sends a message to Diego and Princess that white, middle-class people are the norm, making them less than if they are unable to achieve Ms. Becky's high academic and self-regulatory expectations.

This is a very big contrast to the expectations of the teacher in PreK B. While both classes use the same curriculum, the teachers have different styles and approaches.

PreK B

The teacher of PreK B, Ms. Jane, is an exuberant Caucasian preschool teacher who has worked at Hampton Center for the past seven years. Every time that I visited Ms. Jane's classroom, she was dancing with the students and making positive comments like, "Good job" or "I love the way you try." Ms. Jane grew up in a high need, low income community, much like the one in which she teaches. While the neighborhood has changed significantly since her childhood becoming much less white and working class and more Black, Ms. Jane does not see herself as separate or distinct from the children she teaches. Instead she describes her children in the classroom and the community as her family: Always I feel I'm one of them. We're a family. I think it's how I was raised. I was in an inner city, so most of my friends were black actually, so I don't see it now. I don't even know that I am different I guess (interview, April 17, 2012).

Purpose of Preschool

For Ms. Jane preschool must be about supporting the development of the whole child. In her words, she wants her students "to grow on their terms," yet, she also recognized that she had a responsibility to help ready her Black students for kindergarten as she explains:
To get them (the children) acclimated to a school setting. To introduce them to literacy, reading. To teach them a love of books. And to socialize the children. Making friends. Preschool I think is huge because I want them to love school and to love to learn (interview, April 17, 2012).
Ms. Jane not only wants her children to engage with literacy but also wants her students to gain the self-regulation skills necessary to socialize effectively as well as the skills that will help them to become life-long learners.

To achieve these aims in practice, Ms. Jane, creates the classroom as a space full of literacy experiences to promote prereading and writing skills, a social emotional space that encourages them to express their feelings, and a multicultural space that shows pride in their cultural backgrounds.

Environmental literacy.

One of Ms. Jane's goals as a preschool teacher is "to introduce them to literacy, reading. To teach them a love of books. It's my passion; I love to read" (interview, April 17, 2012). As a consequence, Ms. Jane creates a literacy rich environment by including books throughout the classroom as well as writing implements, picture/word labels, and children's name/vocabulary cards to assist the children in achieving her goals. Every material has a place on an open shelf at the children's eye level or lower with 3X5 labels on the boxes that have a picture of the material and the name of the material. This arrangement and labeling shows the children what is available in each area, and because everything is accessible children are able to choose where and what they would like to play.

Ms. Jane provides a wide variety of books for her students. She has more than fifty books in her library area on any given day, as well as over three hundred more to rotate to match themes. These books consist of fiction, nonfiction, storybooks, as well as books that reflect the children's gender, cultural, racial, and social diversity (Copple & Bredekamp, 2009). Because Ms. Jane feels that literacy is so important, every area of the classroom includes a container of books that relate to the toys in that area, such as *A House for Hermit Crab* in the Discovery Area and *Peter's Chair* in Dramatic Play. Along with the books, there were pictures in each area, labeled with words that the children could use to enhance their vocabulary, such as names of different kinds of vehicles in blocks or new foods in dramatic play. Each area also had writing materials, such as paper, pencils, crayons, markers, dry erase boards, dry erase markers, chalk boards, and chalk, to encourage the children to create letters, books, and lists. There were also laminated cards with the children's names written on them so children could copy the letters in their name and therefore be able to label their own work (Copple & Bredekamp, 2009). For Ms. Jane, literacy is more than just having books present for her students to look at, but about creating a space that, encourages children to try to express their own ideas, and to use writing and reading in purposeful ways.

Social emotional space.

The classroom, while small, has a lot of color and many activities. As in all Creative Curriculum classrooms, there are nine interest areas set up within the classroom: dramatic play, blocks, music and movement, computers, toys and games, discovery, library, art, and sand and water. Each area is set up in a way that allows children to make decisions without needing adult help. For example, each learning center is a designated by a clearly labeled sign with a picture of toys that are available in that area. The physical space set up by Ms. Jane reflects her goal of acclimating children to a school setting. She chooses materials and equipment with the children's developmental levels, interests and social backgrounds in mind, as suggested by developmentally appropriate practices (Copple & Bredekamp, 2009).

Research indicates that educators who establish firm boundaries, foster warm personal relationships in the classroom, and enable students to have an impact on their environment strengthen students' attachment to school, their interest in learning, their ability to refrain from self-destructive behaviors, and their positive behaviors (Elias, Zins, Weissberg, Greenberg, Haynes, Kessler, Schwab-Stone, & Shriver, 1997, p. 44).

Preschool is a time in which teachers are expected to assist children in learning socially appropriate behaviors. Positive decision making consists of many tasks for preschool age children. They must learn to control their impulses, such as hitting when another child takes a toy from them, and to adapt to new sets of rules, such as asking a teacher to take them to the bathroom. In addition, by being in a space with other people aside from their families, children have to learn how to resolve conflicts.

Ms. Jane tries to make this transition to a new set of rules smoother by having the children assist in making decisions. "Student participation in classroom decisions and responsibilities provides an excellent opportunity for them to experience the satisfaction and responsibility of influencing their classroom environment" (Elias et. al., 1997, p. 44). One way of accomplishing this is by having the children participate in creating the classroom rules. The rules for PreK B (see Figure 2) were created by the class as a group during whole group time in September and are displayed on the wall by the carpet. These rules are part of the special give and take of ideas and power that occurs in PreK B because they allow the children to take on a leadership role that is usually reserved for teachers.

Another way this give and take occurs in PreK B is through the introduction of new materials. Instead of telling the children how new materials will be used, Ms. Jane has an open discussion with the children. An example of this occurred at the beginning of the day May 16, 2012, when Ms. Jane took out a new toy during whole group:

Ms. Jane: "Look what I have here for you. Grow a head butterfly bug. I will put it in science." She pointed to the wings and said, "It has…?"

The children: "Wings."

Ms. Jane: "How many legs?"

Children: "Six."

Ms. Jane writes six on the board. Ms. Jane: "We'll water it and it will be what?"

The children: "Hair."

Ms. Jane: "Grass." She puts the butterfly down on the discovery table (observation, May 16, 2012).

In this interaction, Ms. Jane does not negate the children's ideas that there will be hair on the butterfly after they water it. Instead, Ms. Jane allows the students to make their predictions before correcting them; by doing this she gives them a chance to try their ideas without judgment, allowing the children to understand that their opinions are valued. In addition to allowing her students to have some say in classroom issues, Ms. Jane is also aware of the importance of children learning how to regulate their emotions. As she told me during an interview on April 17, 2012:

We have some anger management issues here sometimes. They (children) have hit me. They (children) have temper tantrums. One punched me in the back when I wasn't looking. Sometimes when another gets frustrated, he has pushed and hit me. So those things do happen. But they're just little ones. They don't understand. They're still working out…they're frustrated, and it's my job to teach them how to express it in

a different manner, so I work on that as well.

To assist her students to learn how to process their feelings, Ms. Jane has set up the

classroom space with areas for children to be able to reflect on their feelings and take time away

from the classroom community. In the library area, there is a bean bag chair in a corner with a

label over it that said, "Cozy Corner." In this corner, there is a picture of a child resting next to

the bean bag chair and a poster on the other side of the bean bag chair that showed pictures of

feelings suggesting to children that they can learn to understand and control their feelings, as

well as have a place to comfort themselves when they find that they are angry, sad, shy or tired.

Ms. Jane encourages the children to use the cozy corner to relax when they become

overwhelmed or frustrated. In addition to this cozy corner, there is a "work it out table" set up for

children who are angry where Ms. Jane has set up a container of play dough and a soft chair with

a few pillows. These materials encourage children to work through their anger and frustration.

Ms. Jane told me on June 5, 2012, "I added special books about working through anger when the

children became frustrated and began fighting last month." Children's books, along with adding

materials to work out frustration, modeling the appropriate use of these materials and teaching

lessons on social/emotional issues, teachers are able to assist preschool students in learning

prosocial behaviors such as sharing and empathy as well as respect and justice (Copple &

Bredekamp, 2009).

A multi-cultural space.

"Culturally relevant teaching uses student culture in order to maintain it and to transcend

the negative effects of dominant culture" (Ladson-Billings, 1994, p. 17). Ms. Jane creates a classroom that supported not only the children's social and emotional growth but also recognized and validated their cultural identities. By presenting children with a space that is full of materials that reflect their cultures, they are more likely to feel comfortable and accepted, making it easier for them to achieve in the classroom. Every interest area in PreK B has some multicultural materials. In the dramatic play area, the toys include dolls from a variety of racial backgrounds, clothing from different ethnicities, pictures of various types of families, and play food from different cultures; there are also a number of books available in that area with such topics as making friends, families, foods, and children with different abilities. Students have brought in flags from their families' countries of origin as well as native costumes. Some of these countries include Nigeria, Jamaica, Barbados, and the Bahamas. The flags of these countries are on display on the walls of dramatic play, and the costumes are available as dress up clothes.

While the block area has the expected unit blocks, Ms. Jane also included plastic figures of people of varying ages, ethnicities, and abilities. There are also books in the block area that depict buildings from around the world such as Big Ben, the Taj Mahal, and the Eiffel Tower. The library includes puppets of varying skin tones and felt board pieces from stories such as *Peter's Chair* and *Anasai the Spider*, as well as books from different African countries and cultures (e.g., African American culture, African tribal cultures, and the Caribbean island cultures). Since all the children in this class are Black, these books hold some meaning for them. Peter, the main character in *Peter's Chair* by Ezra Jack Keats is a Black boy living in an urban setting, similar to the one in which the children of PreK B live. *Anasai the Spider* depicts traditional African motifs, which shows children from African backgrounds some ideas about the rich culture of their ancestors.

Ms. Jane uses her classroom space to achieve her goals of facilitating children's autonomy, and socio-emotional development and encouraging them to read and write and does so in a way that attempts to recognize the cultures of her students.

Ms. Jane's teaching.

Child-centered education is an idea that dates back to the era of Progressive education and that has been taken up in the psychological theories of Piaget and Vygotsky. Viewed by the field as best practice and described in the concept of developmentally appropriate practices (Copple & Bredekamp, 2009), child centered approaches were the cornerstone of Ms. Jane's teaching.

According to Dewey, there are two criteria for an educative experience, continuity and interaction. Continuity describes how an experience if it is to be educative must build on and extend what has come before, rather than simply be more of the same. Interaction describes the aspects of the experience as they relate to the environment in which the experience occurred as well as to the students' past experiences, making each interaction unique for each individual (Dewey, 1997). Therefore, there is no lesson that has intrinsic value because value comes from the experiences of the people participating in the lesson. This concept of experience encourages educators to take cues from the children, following their interests for lesson planning and discussions. Children have their own knowledge and need to have experiences to engage and expand this knowledge.

Like Dewey, Piaget argued that children construct knowledge by coming into contact with new information through their interaction with objects and experiences. "Piaget concluded that the essential nature of human beings was their power to construct knowledge through adaptation to the environment" (Williams, 1999, p. 13). To adapt and create more complex understandings, Piaget argued that children engage in the processes of assimilation and accommodation which are fueled by children's interactions. In assimilation, children try to match new objects and experiences to their existing schema, such as a child who has a dog might mistakenly call a cat, dog the first time s/he sees one. In accommodation, children create new categories for new objects and experiences.

The ideas of assimilation and accommodation are important to keep in mind when teaching children in whole group because some children may be focusing on the task of assimilation, still matching new experiences into their existing schema, while others are readily accommodating the new information into new categories; thus it can be confusing and overwhelming for some children if a teacher moves to quickly from one theme to another when they have not yet created a category for that concept. Likewise, children who are readily accommodating information may be bored if a single theme is presented in a single manner for too long of a period of time because they are ready for a new challenge.

One way children learn and build knowledge through interaction is in play. Play stimulates abstract thinking through role play; children take on roles in an effort to resolve problems, such as acting as a mother who is punishing a doll for dropping dinner dishes. According to Vygotsky, it is through this type of imaginative play that children are able to learn more about themselves and the world around them.

These theoretical ideas are brought together in the guidelines for developmentally appropriate practice (Copple & Bredekamp, 2009), the fields' consensus definition of best practice. An effective education is one that builds on children's experiences, allows them opportunities to interact with their environment and uses play teach children to not only enjoy school but to learn preliteracy skills, math skills, and prosocial behavior. This child centered pedagogy requires that teachers pay attention to the individual development of each child, while balancing academics with the children's need to play (Copple & Bredekamp, 2009). Ms. Jane looked to the children's needs and experiences to dictate what she should teach. This included the studies and themes as well as the length of time that she focused on those lessons through large and small groups. While Ms. Jane enacted a developmentally appropriate approach, she was not always as culturally responsive in her teaching, overlooking teachable moments that existed for her Black students.

Whole Group

Whole group, or circle time as it is called in many curricula, "is a period of class activity, in which pupils and teacher sit together in a circle formation, to share ideas, feelings and games/activities about one or more social/emotional/curricular issues" (Lown, 2002, p. 93). Lown's very broad idea is typically seen in the guise of the morning meeting in which preschool teachers greet students, go through the calendar, look at the weather, sing songs, and read a message or book. Whole group does not seem like a time when a teacher can be child-centered because it is typically structured as an adult-led and created instructional event. However, the way Ms. Jane structured her whole group, during each of the four whole groups I observed, was very much about a give and take between her and the children.

Ms. Jane has several tasks that she tries to accomplish each day during whole group time, as indicated on her lesson plans: morning song, counting the children, weather bunny/butterfly, morning message (usually just the date), and a song. Whole group time in PreK B lasts between five and ten minutes. The following vignette shows what a typical whole group time looks like in

PreK B. As this vignette begins, the children are playing with the dollhouse and table toys before going to whole group:

Ms. Jane: "One more minute until we start our day." "Alright. We'll put on our morning song." (She begins to dance to the music.)

The children smile and walk to the carpet to dance with Ms. Jane.

The song ends. Ms. Jane turns off the CD player and sits on the carpet for whole group.

Ms. Jane: "Alright. Find your spots please. No squishy squashy please." When all the children sit down, Ms. Jane begins to count the children. Several children count with her: ""1, 2, 3, 4, 5, 6, 7, 8, 9, 10, 11, 12, 13. Uno, dos, tres, cuatro, cinco, seis, seite, ocho, neuve, diez, once, doce, trece." Ms. Jane looks at the children: "Who's not here?"

The children: "Gabby and Mark."

Ms. Jane points to the 15 on her number chart with her pointer, moving the pointer as the children count each number: "15, 14, 13, 12, 11, 10, 9, 8, 7, 6, 5, 4, 3, 2, 1, blast off!"

Several children count aloud with Ms. Jane: "15, 14, 13, 12, 11, 10, 9, 8, 7, 6, 5, 4, 3, 2, 1, blast off!" Then, Ms. Jane looks around the circle, points to a butterfly headband: "It's time for the weather butterfly."

Tara puts on the headband, walks to the window: "Sunny."

The children: "Thank you weather butterfly." Everyone claps.

Ms. Jane: "Close your eyes," as she erases the board. "What did we talk about yesterday?" The children open their eyes.

Then, all the children: "Our butterflies."

Children begin to call out. No one raises hands.

Tara: "They hatch soon."

Jay: "I want to see."

Linda: "Mine will fly."

Ms. Jane", "Yes." Then, she begins to write on the dry erase board.

"Left to right."

Ms. Jane writes, June 14, 2012. She spells: "J U N E."

The children repeat: "J U N E."

Ms. Jane: "June 14, 2012."

The children repeat: "June 14, 2012."

Then, everyone sings the color song as they get ready to go outside

(observation, June 14, 2012).

While this was the typical whole group format, I did not observe two whole group times

that were the same because Ms. Jane modified the instructional event to meet the needs of the

children. Ms. Jane's child centered approach to large group instruction was evident in two ways:

taking cues from children and engaging in conversation during whole group.

Taking cues from children.

To be child-centered means to take cues from children, both the group of children one

teaches and individuals who may need attention. Ms. Jane was always aware of the needs of her

individual students and adapted her schedule to respond to the cues they sent. This flexibility was

evident for example on April, 17, 2012 when Ty, who was feeling a little uncomfortable, walked into the classroom late when morning meeting had already begun. Although Ms. Jane was sitting on the carpet in a circle with the children, Ms. Jane got up, walked over and hugged Ty; then quickly walked back to her seat on the carpet. In response, Ty came and sat on the carpet (observation, April, 17, 2012).

Similarly, Ms. Jane changed her plans to accommodate the attention span of her young students:

> The children had been sitting on the carpet with Ms. Jane for about five minutes. The sun is shining into the windows. Eleven children are sitting on the rug.
>
> Ms. Jane: "What are we learning about?" She holds up a book with a picture of an ant.
>
> Ty: "Ant."
>
> Ms. Jane: "What does the queen ant do?"
>
> Bink: "Eggs."
>
> Ty, pointing to the picture of the ant in the book: "These are eggs and this has six legs."
>
> Ms. Jane repeats Ty's words for the class.
>
> Six of the children lie down and roll on the carpet, bumping into each other and into the children who are looking at the book.
>
> Ms. Jane: "Would you like to read the book later?'
>
> A few children nod their heads.
>
> Ms. Jane puts the book away: "Children it is now time for gross motor Exercise." (observation, May 2, 2012).

As Ms. Jane is getting ready to read a book, she noticed that some children were not engaged. Instead of reprimanding or redirecting them to sit up and pay attention, Ms. Jane takes this as a signal that the children have had enough of whole group for the moment and need more time outside. While this tactic is developmentally appropriate and meets the needs of young children's attention span, it may not help prepare the low-income, Black children in Ms. Jane's class for success in a society in which the norms tend to marginalize their needs, not strive to accommodate and anticipate them.

Looking across the four whole group times, there was always some continuity such as going through the calendar and counting backwards, but Ms. Jane made sure to include time for the children.

Encouraging conversation.

Studies of teacher-child interaction in whole class instruction have found that the teacher controls the tone and focus of the conversation (Lown, 2002) because the teacher is the one who chooses the topic, runs the classroom, and is sitting in the front of the whole group; Ms. Jane, on the other hand, shares control of whole group with the students, allowing their ideas to shift the focus of the conversation. Rather children are allowed to offer their contributions and to add on to each other's answers. For example, in the following whole group on May 16 the children end up having an extended conversation about caterpillars and eggs:

Ms. Jane and the children sit on the carpet in the whole group area.

The children sit on the outer edge of the carpet. All children have a clear

view of Ms. Jane as she holds up a book. Ms. Jane shows a books and

points to the pictures. First, she shows the cover. Then, she shows the first page: "That's an egg. I will read it over again. *Butterfly Mariposa.* How do butterflies grow? From egg to caterpillar."

Derek: "That's a caterpillar."

Tara: "I want to touch a caterpillar."

Linda: "It was egg."

Sara: "We gonna have caterpillars."

Ms. Jane: "Our caterpillar should be here any day. I'm waiting for them to come."

Derek: "I like caterpillars."

Tara: "How bout I can touch it?"

Ms. Jane: "I don't know if we'll touch them. Real gently maybe."

Sara: "I love the green ones."

Ms. Jane as she shows the second page: "From caterpillar to chrysalis."

Maria smiles as she looks at the book.

Dora: "Another caterpillar."

Bink: "Whoa!"

Derek: "What's inside?"

Ms. Jane shows the third: "And from chrysalis to…"

Jeff: "It's coming to a butterfly."

Ms. Jane shows the last page of the book.

Tara and Sara: "Butterfly" (observation, May 16, 2012).

As can be seen, Ms. Jane does not negate children's ideas and gives authority mostly over to the children without letting the conversations get out of hand. For example, when Tara says, "How bout I can touch it." Ms. Jane does not say no, she says, "I don't know if we'll touch them. Real gently maybe." She leaves the possibility open for Tara. At the same time, Ms. Jane adds information that helps keep the conversations moving in productive ways. When Derek asks, "What's inside?," Ms. Jane shows the next page of the book instead of answering his question outright, giving Derek a chance to discover the knowledge on his own; she simply reads the text, "And from chrysalis to…" Ms. Jane allows her students to take control of coming up with the answers to the questions that they have by showing them how to find the answers; this leads the children to stay on the topic that Ms. Jane has chosen to meet the needs of her lesson.

In most of the whole group times that I observed, Ms. Jane encouraged conversation, even during routine tasks. When taking attendance on April 17, during whole group time, Ms. Jane's students were eager to help:

> Ms. Jane walks to the children's home/school board that the
>
> children sign in on during free play and points to the board with her
>
> pointer: "Who is missing?"
>
> Jay: "Dora, Ben, Ty"
>
> Gabby: "Linda, Paje."
>
> Bink: "Maria" (observation, April 17, 2012).

In this brief vignette, the conversational tone of whole group time could be seen in a simple question. Many teachers ask "Who is missing?," but they expect the children to wait to be called on. Ms. Jane allowed her students to engage in the natural flow of conversation by answering her question as they saw fit, and they, in turn, respected her and each other by taking turns speaking. Ms. Jane's conversation technique is child-centered, but the conversation still remains on the topic that she planned.

Similarly, on June 14, when Ms. Jane asked the children to remember what they were learning about, a conversation ensued:

> Ms. Jane: "Close your eyes," as she erases the board. "What did we talk about yesterday?" The children open their eyes."

> Then, all the children: "Our butterflies."

> Children begin to call out. No one raises hands.

> Tara: "They hatch soon."

> Jay: "I want to see."

> Linda: "Mine will fly."

> Ms. Jane: "Yes." Then, she begins to write the date on the dry erase board (observation, June 14, 2012).

Again, though the children call out, they do not speak over each other. They listen to the person who is speaking before beginning to talk. The calling out is in fact a conversation in which the children add to each other's ideas. When Tara says, "They will hatch soon," Jay add, "I want to see." Taken in context these comments create a full conversation about the butterflies that they are remembering, but the conversation stays firmly on the topic of caterpillars and butterflies without wavering, which leaves the observer to wonder what is not being said by the students, especially those who do not speak up during whole group.

Another way Ms. Jane made sure children's voices were heard in large group was by deliberately planning for their input. For example, the plans for Ms. Jane's whole group time included "complimentary remarks said from classmates;" Ms. Jane said that this meant that children could contribute anything they thought was relevant to the topic (interview, June 14, 2012). Also, on her lesson plans, Ms. Jane indicated that the children chose the books for afternoon read aloud. In the interview on June 24, 2012, she said, "This is another way that the children can contribute their opinions on what they want to learn about" (interview, June 14, 2012).

Allowing for these complimentary remarks could be seen on June 14, when the children discussed their butterflies:

Ms. Jane: "Close your eyes," as she erases the board. "What did

we talk about yesterday?" The children open their eyes."

Then all the children: "Our butterflies."

Children begin to call out. No one raises hands.

Tara: "They hatch soon."

Jay: "I want to see."

Linda: "Mine will fly."

Ms. Jane: "Yes." Then, she begins to write the date on the dry

erase board (observation, June 14, 2012).

Ms. Jane starts the discussion, but does not interrupt the children, allowing their ideas to flow into one another inspiring others to join the conversation.

Similarly, "complimentary remarks said from classmates" also occurred on May 16, when the children were talking about caterpillars:

Derek: "That's a caterpillar.

Tara: "I want to touch a caterpillar."

Linda: "It was egg."

Sara: "We gonna have caterpillars."

Ms. Jane: "Our caterpillar should be here any day. I'm waiting for

them to come."

Derek: "I like caterpillars."

Tara: "How bout I can touch it?"

Ms. Jane: "I don't know if we'll touch them. Real gently maybe."

Sara: "I love the green ones" (observation, May 16, 2012).

Despite the caterpillars not having arrived in the classroom as yet, Ms. Jane welcomes the

children's interest, adding to the conversation. In doing so, the children know that their views

will be validated. By allowing for "complimentary remarks from classmates," Ms. Jane adapts

her teaching to match the interests of her students.

Ms. Jane's dialogic style with the children is reminiscent of the "involvement style" of

communication that Hallum (2006) states is more aligned with African American students' style

of communication in which they are free to add to another's statement or answer in order to

enhance the conversation. By bouncing ideas off one another, Ms. Jane acts as a participant in

the conversation, not a leader, which helps to build trusting relationships between the children

and Ms. Jane because they learn that she values their opinions. However, Ms. Jane is still

controlling the focus of the conversation, not allowing the children to fully express their

interests, backgrounds, or cultures. So, there is a give and take, but the content of the

conversations is still Ms. Jane's, for the most part, which when I was observing was mostly

about insects.

By allowing for the children to have some control over the interactions and questions,

Ms. Jane shared the control of knowledge during whole group. By planning for these shared interactions in her lesson plans and in her talk and actions, Ms. Jane let the children know that she valued the knowledge that they brought into the classroom. This is the child-study that Dewey was envisioning in *The Child and the Curriculum*, where the child is taken at his or her own present level of consciousness and not just thought of in terms of what they have accomplished but in what they think about (Dewey, 2011).

Studies of the differences between schools serving mostly Black and poor students and those serving predominantly white populations tend to find a lot of teacher control of whole group conversation, such as in Ms. Becky's classroom, with this instructional event emphasizing drill and rote memorization of academic concepts. For example, in Lubeck's (1985) study of a Black Head Start classroom, the Black teachers said they used whole group to have children gather for rote drills of calendar, story reading, and roll call. While Ms. Jane is teaching a similar population of students, her whole group time is much more of a conversation between herself and her students.

At the same time, while there was a give and take, Ms. Jane always kept whole group focused on her agenda and the topics she raised, which did not extend to the backgrounds or cultures of the children in the classroom. Delpit (2006) would argue that this discourse style is a middle-class approach that negates what young Black children need to be able to succeed in school.

Interactions with Focal Children

In PreK B, small group is a very individualized experience in that Ms. Jane typically works one-on-one with students to accomplish her learning goals rather than in a small group. Over my weeks in the classroom, I actually never saw Ms. Jane do small group any other way than as one on one with the two focal children. Therefore, in this section, I begin by describing Ms. Jane's plans for small group and then examine how she taught these concepts and skills individually to each of the focal children Bink and Dora.

Small group curriculum.

Small group is a time to work with children on the skills that they need to improve as working with fewer children enables the teacher to individualize instruction. As Ms. Jane explained during an interview, "I just want them to grow on their terms" (interview, April, 12, 2012), which can be accomplished during small group through differentiated instruction. Since Ms. Jane has chosen to differentiate instruction for every student, Ms. Jane creates one activity for small group each week and then she rotates each child through this activity while the other children are in choice time. Ms. Jane said that she uses her observations to let her know what academic focus each child needs to work on during small group (interview, June 14, 2012). Ms. Jane uses the theme to focus her conversation and interactions with each child during these individual interactions. Ms. Jane stated in an interviewed conducted on June 14, 2012 that she derived the themes from the children's interests as assessed from the anecdotes that she writes down during class. However, she did not provide any examples of a theme that came from the children nor did I find any examples of the themes based on what was recorded in the anecdotal records. Ultimately, it was Ms. Jane who chose the themes for the lessons. Ms. Jane planned each of her small groups to match the theme of the week, so the lessons were on plants and insects when I was observing in her classroom. The goals for each small group are academic, either literacy or math based. The focus for the small group observations can be found in Table 1.

Table 1 – Small Group Observation Focuses for PreK B

Date	Theme	Focus	Activity
4/24/12	Plants	How seeds grow – describing words	Looking at seedlings and describing them
5/10/12	Bugs	Patterns	Plastic bug toys
5/23/12	Caterpillars	Counting	Caterpillar face and circles
6/8/12	Caterpillars	Reading Comprehension	Storybook read aloud

The academic focus of the first activity, how seeds grow, was choosing adjectives and descriptive phrases that enhance language to explain what was previously discussed, preparing the children to learn about grammar. This activity was question based, and Ms. Jane focused on building on the children's experience of planting the seeds through leading questions. For bugged out patterns, the second activity, the focus was continuing two color patterns. The academic focus of the third activity, caterpillar circles, was counting. For *The Very Hungry Caterpillar*, the fourth activity, the skill being addressed was story retelling,

Within each of these activities, Ms. Jane used her relationship with the individual children to hone in on a particular academic goal for each child. To create the individualized interactions, Ms. Jane looks over the anecdotal records she created during the week and uses those to guide her choices of learning objectives from Creative Curriculum to teach to each child. In her observation notes, Ms. Jane noted that on February 24, 2012, "Dora could not pattern," so

Ms. Jane set up the Bugged Out patterns lesson on May 10, 2012 to work on this skill with Dora. This does not mean that Ms. Jane created a different small group experience for each child each week since Bink also worked on the Bugged Out patterns lesson; but she used her anecdotes to help her choose how to approach the lesson with each student and what the goal of the lesson should be. Ms. Jane approached each of these lessons in a manner that would allow her to be student focused, but when looking at the individual children involved in these lessons, it becomes clear that Ms. Jane put her academic goals of these lessons above the needs of the children for whom the lessons were intended.

Dora.

Dora comes to school smiling almost every day. She was born in the low-income housing project that she still lives in with her mother, grandmother, and two sisters. Her father is from Liberia and visits two or three times a month. She is one of the taller children in PreK B and usually wears her hair in many braids. Her favorite outfits to wear to school are jeans, sneakers and pink t-shirts. However, I was never certain how I'd find Dora attired for the day as when I came to visit on a day when it was eighty degrees, Dora was wearing corduroys and a sweatshirt. Another day when I came it visit, it was only sixty degrees, and Dora was wearing shorts, a tank top, and sandals.

Ms. Jane sees Dora as a bright child, who is eager to please. When asked to describe Dora, she said, "Dora is another one, very affectionate, very happy too, follows me around. Eager to learn. Dora is a happy child too" (interview, June 15, 2012). Sometimes, Dora gets very shy and does not like to speak. According to the Family Conference form dated April 16, 2012, Ms. Jane is working with Dora on her confidence and focus. Although she had noted this goal of confidence building with Dora, Ms. Jane's focus with her in the small groups I observed seemed to be about more academic goals, such as patterning and story retelling. While these interactions could allow for more give and take between Ms. Jane and Dora, in her interactions with Dora the focus was on ensuring that Dora gave the correct, expected answers with Ms. Jane leading Dora's responses as in the following interaction:

Ms. Jane calls Dora over to the library and shows her the book, *The Very Hungry Caterpillar*. Ms. Jane: "Do you remember this book?"

Dora nods.

Ms. Jane: "Can you tell me about this book? Let's open up to the beginning of the book?" Ms. Jane holds the book open to the first page.

Dora: "That one is the caterpillar. No, it the moon."

Ms. Jane: "We don't see the caterpillar yet do we?"

Dora turns the page: "Caterpillar."

Ms. Jane: "And he popped out of the little?"

Dora: "Egg. Let's find the strawberries." Dora flips through the pages. "He eat the strawberry. He eat the apples. He eat the oranges."

Ms. Jane points to the picture of the apples on the page that Dora is looking at: "How many apples?"

Dora: "1."

Ms. Jane points to the picture of the pears: "How many pears?"

Dora: "1 2."

Ms. Jane points to the plums: "How many plums?"

Dora: "1."

Ms. Jane: "Would you like to count with me?"

Dora nods.

Ms. Jane points to each plum and counts with Dora: "1 2 3."

Ms. Jane: "Good job."

Then, they count the strawberries and oranges together.

Dora turns the page: "He eat sausage. He eat a cheese. He eat a ice cream. He eat a lollipop. He eat a cupcake. He eat a watermelon."

Ms. Jane: "What happened after he ate all that food?"

Dora: "He got a tummy ache."

Ms. Jane: "Why do you think he has a stomachache?"

Dora: "Cause he eat a lollipop."

Ms. Jane: "He ate a lot of food and a lollipop was one of the things."

Dora turns the page: "He eat a flowers."

Ms. Jane: "What did he eat?"

Dora: "He eat a flower."

Ms. Jane: "It's like a flower it's a leaf. After he ate the leaf, he felt?"

Dora: "Better."

Ms. Jane: "They he started to get?"

Dora: "Bigger."

Ms. Jane: "Then he built a little house called a…"

Dora: "Chrysalis."

Ms. Jane: "We have chrysalis in discovery. They're turning into…"

Dora: "Butterfly."

Ms. Jane: "Thank you" (observation, June 8, 2012).

In this vignette, Dora does not seem to want to go through the story a page at a time. She rushes from the beginning to her favorite part with the strawberry as soon as she gets a hold of the book. Then, Ms. Jane slows her down, only allowing her to control the conversation twice, which does not match with the goal that Ms. Jane has set for Dora. The first time occurs when Dora is looking for the page with the strawberries "Let's find the strawberries." Dora flips through the pages. "He eat the strawberry. He eat the apples. He eat the oranges." In the second instance, Dora has just finished counting pictures with Ms. Jane and chooses to look through the next page on her own: Dora turns the page: "He eat sausage. He eat a cheese. He eat a ice cream. He eat a lollipop. He eat a cupcake. He eat a watermelon." Telling the story by memory and picture the way Dora is participating in is an important literacy skill, retelling her own version of the story. Story retelling is one way for young children to improve their reading comprehension and show their understanding of the story that has been read to them. Children use their own words, based in memories and the pictures in the book, to explain the story. However, Ms. Jane does not allow Dora to retell her own version of the story; Dora is persuaded by Ms. Jane to only retell Ms. Jane's version of the story.

Ms. Jane chooses to make the section of *The Very Hungry Caterpillar* that contains different fruits into a counting lesson, while Dora wanted to look at her favorite page. For children who are developing emergent reading skills, having a favorite part of a book is important because that child is developing a love of reading, which Ms. Jane claims is one of her key teaching aims (interview, April 17, 2012). Ms. Jane does not seem to notice that she has taken over the section that Dora was most excited about. This is a missed opportunity to allow Dora to share her knowledge and understanding of the story. Dora however gives in and relinquishes ownership of the story to Ms. Jane for the rest of the book, simply answering what is asked of her. Although Ms. Jane does meet some of the literacy standards, such as book handling skills and having a child exhibit reading-like behavior, she missed out on three opportunities to capitalize on Dora's enthusiasm about this book.

In the next example, Ms. Jane follows a similar pattern of leading Dora through the answers to her questions about seedlings:

> Ms. Jane has two egg cartons of seedlings on the table; she asks Dora to come to the table to play.
>
> Ms. Jane: "We were talking about our seeds today in whole group. Can you tell me more about our seeds? What did you say about them in whole group?"
>
> Dora: "Them grow."
>
> Ms. Jane: "They grow. How do they grow?"
>
> Dora: "With water."
>
> Ms. Jane: "Right. What do you see out of the seeds, sweetie?"
>
> Dora: "Them grow into jellybeans."
>
> Ms. Jane laughs: "They're shaped like jellybeans, aren't they. And out of the seeds, what is that?"
>
> Dora: "The roots."
>
> Ms. Jane: "That's right, the roots. What do the roots do?"
>
> Dora: "To keep the flowers so they grow."

Ms. Jane: "Exactly. What does it drink up?"

Dora: "Water."

Ms. Jane: "Can you count how many seeds?"

Dora: "1 2 3 4 5 6 7 8 9 10 11 12 13 14 16 17 18 19 20 21 22 23 24 25."

She points to each seedling as she counted.

Ms. Jane: "Good job. I love the way you count and recognize the

numbers" (observation, April 24, 2013).

During this interaction Ms. Jane laughs at Dora when her response does not answer the question

that she is asking. Instead of probing to see what it is that Dora is getting at when she says,

"Them grow into jellybeans." Ms. Jane assumes that Dora means that the seeds look like

jellybeans without giving her time to explain. By not encouraging Dora to explain herself, Ms.

Jane is not meeting her own goal of getting Dora to speak more during class but more

importantly, she seems to be only looking for the correct answer to her questions. For the most

part Dora is able to answer these questions and performs well, but Ms. Jane has also missed out

on learning more about Dora.

The following lesson, a counting lesson, shows a similar pattern of interaction between

Ms. Jane and Dora. Ms. Jane placed a circle with a face on the table in front of Dora and a pile of

laminated circles with the intention of building a caterpillar. Together, they added circles after

the face to create a caterpillar. Then, Ms. Jane and Dora counted the circles:

Dora counts and Ms. Jane repeats the numbers she says. She puts

her hand over hers and guides it to touch each circle as she counts. "1, 2,

3, 4, 5, 6, 7, 8."

Ms. Jane: "Good job. You wanna make him bigger?"

Dora smiles and nods.

Ms. Jane: "Go ahead."

Dora adds several circles to the back of the caterpillar.

As Dora adds circles, Ms. Jane: "He's been eating a lot. He's

getting bigger. Okay. Wowee. Wow. Let's stop right there." Ms. Jane

takes the caterpillar pieces apart and writes down notes in her notebook.

Then, Dora chooses an area on the choice board (observation, May 23,

2012).

For the most part Dora is a silent participant in this small group. During this interaction, Dora

only counts aloud once, even though she showed that she was able to count to 25 without

assistance on April 24, 2012. Dora continued to perform the task chosen by Ms. Jane but would

not answer any of her questions aloud. Ms. Jane, however, was not dissuaded by Dora's silence;

she continued the activity speaking for both of them when Dora does not verbally respond.

However, one of Ms. Jane's goals for Dora is for her to speak out more. This interaction does not

achieve Ms. Jane's goals for Dora and looks to be just filling time during the school day to make

sure that all children have done this activity.

Ms. Jane's focus on ensuring that Dora gave the correct, expected answers leads Ms. Jane

to direct Dora through tasks even when the concept of the task is beyond Dora's comprehension.

As can be seen in this lesson where the focus is on patterning with two colors:

Ms. Jane places red, blue, and green rectangular bug toys on the

table; she arranges the bug toys into a pattern of red blue red blue and

invites Dora over to the table. Dora stands next to the table as Ms. Jane

begins to speak to her.

Ms. Jane: "Red, blue, red, blue. What do you think comes next?"

Dora sits next to Ms. Jane in the toys and games area, staring at the pattern on the table without speaking.

Ms. Jane: "Can you pick out which color comes next?"

Dora looks at Ms. Jane without speaking.

Ms. Jane: "Red, blue, red, blue. Is it red or is it blue?" She uses her finger to point to each color as she says its name.

Dora: "That," and picks a blue bug.

Ms. Jane: "Let me show you something. Red blue red blue next comes red. You see they're different colors and they're taking turns."

Ms. Jane points to a red bug: "What color's this one?"

Dora: "Yellow."

Ms. Jane: "Red." Then she points to a blue bug: "What color's that one?"

Dora looks, but does not speak.

Ms. Jane: "Blue."

Dora: "Blue" (observation, May 10, 2012).

Ms. Jane was clearly assuming that the children remembered learning the colors and was not looking to reteach this concept. However, Dora does not know either of the two colors that Ms. Jane used to create patterns for this lesson, but Ms. Jane does not stop the lesson to teach Dora about the colors. Ms. Jane did not take any observation notes about Dora's sorting and classifying from September 12, 2011 through May 3, 2012. Therefore, I am not sure how she would know if Dora was capable of classifying colors before working on this patterning lesson.

What is also concerning is that Ms. Jane is not teaching this foundational skill to Dora but instead persists with the lesson when Dora clearly does not know her colors.

Ms. Jane's interactions with Dora show a teacher who chooses materials that her student has shown interest in, but who has a specific agenda that must be completed during each interaction. It is clear in the interaction with the colored bugs (May 10, 2012) that Dora does not know how to identify colors, but Ms. Jane had determined that the time needed to be used for patterning. Instead of focusing on the differences between the colors and changing the lesson, Ms. Jane simply gave Dora the answers to the lesson, having her repeat the names of the colors. When the focus of Ms. Jane's interaction with Dora is a discussion about how plants grow on April 24, 2012, she does not take the time to assist Dora with her grammar or explore the interesting idea that Dora has about plants looking like jellybeans because those are not on the agenda. Likewise, the reason for Dora's silence during the interaction on May 23, 2012 is not brought into question because it does not have to do with building a caterpillar out of a pile of circles. In not addressing Dora's silence, or Dora's inability to identify colors in a pattern, Ms. Jane is not being child-centered and is also not achieving her agenda of academic learning. Ms. Jane decided that Dora is a bright student and led her through lessons in such a way that her observations would show that she was capable of the intended goal of each lesson. Unfortunately, there is minimal concern as to whether Dora is actually learning the material because she is a quiet, low-income, Black female.

Bink.

Bink was born in Jamaica and came to the United States when he was an infant. His parents are still learning American English, as is Bink. They all speak Patois at home, which leads to Bink having some difficulty with speech, according to Ms. Jane (interview, May 15, 2012). Currently, Bink lives with his mother and father in the low-income housing projects, but he rarely sees his father because he spends most of the day and night driving a taxi cab. Bink gravitates towards the music area when he comes into the classroom.

Ms. Jane sees him as struggling academically due to lack of focus, but a hard worker. In her words, "Bink loves music, always happy, and he's very affectionate. A joy to have. Bink is eager to learn too, but Bink has a harder time focusing. He gets distracted easily, so I spend a lot of time trying to get his attention" (interview, June 15, 2012). In the Spring Family Conference Form for Bink, Ms. Jane stated, "Bink may not always seem to pay attention, but he is at the developmental level for his age." He is very good at color identification and patterns, but has trouble with counting, number identification, and letter identification (April 16, 2012). Overall, Ms. Jane expects Bink to answer in incomplete sentences, get distracted, and need help completing a task, which is a concern because she does not take into account Bink's status as an English language learner or the knowledge that Bink might have, which may be due in part to the district not providing English as a second language support for preschool students. Instead in all of her interactions with Bink, in small group, Ms. Jane can be seen trying to focus his attention on her academic goals as in the following lesson on seeds:

Ms. Jane has the two egg cartons of seedlings on the table. Ms.

Jane: "We talked about seeds. What happened to the seeds?"

Bink: "Growing."

Ms. Jane: "They're growing. Why are they growing?"

Bink: "Because."

Ms. Jane: "Because why. Why are they growing?"

Bink: "Because it needs sun and water."

Ms. Jane: "It does need water and sun, excellent." Then, she points

to the roots of the seedling: "What's this?"

Bink: "I don't know."

Ms. Jane: "Roots."

Bink: "Roots."

Ms. Jane: "What are the roots for?"

Bink: "Because grow."

Ms. Jane: "Because it makes it grow. Right, do you know how it

makes it grow? It likes to drink what?"

Bink: "Water."

Ms. Jane: "Yes, sweetie" (observation, April 24, 2012).

As can be seen, Ms. Jane led Bink through the conversation in the above vignette. When Bink

became confused during the lessons, Ms. Jane would prompt him for an answer or give him a

verbal cue that he could repeat. In an interview Ms. Jane said she used this method because, "If

you ask him a direct question, he just laughs. He doesn't answer" (interview, May 15, 2012). She

seems to be trying to work on the New Jersey Preschool Teaching and Learning Standard

"Teachers will extend children's language by asking them to make connections between present

knowledge and new vocabulary" (2009). However, Ms. Jane places her words in Bink's mouth

so that he is unable to express what he knows in his own words. This foreshadows how Bink

may be treated by other teachers who do not understand his unique background as a low-income,

Black immigrant who is an English language learner. Ms. Jane's focus on the correct use of

sentences blinds her to Bink's understanding of the concept of how roots help plants. The inability to construct proper English sentences should not immediately be seen by Ms. Jane as a deficit because English is not Bink's first language, as Delpit (2006) states, "teachers need to support the language that students bring to school, provide them input from an additional code, and give them the opportunity to use the code in a nonthreatening, real communicative context." The way Ms. Jane feeds Bink words, does not allow him to use the academic discourse that he needs to learn to be successful in school.

Similarly, Ms. Jane's seeing Bink as a student who only lacks focus and is not struggling with academics creates a problematic system in which she encourages him without correcting him. Her over encouraging and under correcting of Bink could be seen on May 23, 2012 when Bink struggled with counting:

Ms. Jane uses laminated circles to allow the children to create their own caterpillars. She has a pile of circles sitting on the table when Bink sits down. Ms. Jane places a circle with a face on the table. Then, Ms. Jane and Bink add circles to the back of the caterpillar face.

Ms. Jane: "Alright my friend, are you ready to count the caterpillar body?"

Bink nods. He counts as Ms. Jane guides his finger to touch each circle: "1, 2, 3, 4, 5, 6, 7, 8." Ms. Jane: "Great. Let's make him bigger."

Bink and Ms. Jane add more circles.

When they stop, Ms. Jane: "Are you ready, love?"

Bink smiles. Bink touches the circles as he counts: "1, 3, 4."

Ms. Jane: "Let's start again." She puts her hand over his and guides him to point to each circle individually.

Bink: "1, 2, 3, 4, 5, 6, 7, 8, 9, 10, 14, 16."

Ms. Jane: "Wow. That's not easy to count like that. Could you show me the numerals?" She holds up the number line. "You counted to ten. 1, 2, 3, 4, 5, 6, 7, 8, 9, 10. You did that" She points to each numeral as she says its name: "Can you show me that you know what some of the numbers look like? Can you show me what number two looks like? Can you point to number two, sweetheart?"

Bink points to 3.

Ms. Jane: "That's number 3. Good try. Can you show me number 1?"

Bink points to 4.

Ms. Jane: "That's number 4. Good try. Can you show me number 2?"

Bink points to 6.

Ms. Jane: "That's number 6. Good try. Thank you so much"

(observation, May 23, 2012).

When looking at the above vignette, the fact that Ms. Jane ignored how Bink counted after ten bothered me because it seemed like she was implying that he was only capable of counting to ten. Bink counted: "1, 2, 3, 4, 5, 6, 7, 8, 9, 10, 14, 16." Ms. Jane did not correct the counting, instead she said, "Wow. That's not easy to count like that." In the above interaction, Ms. Jane does not assist Bink to notice the flaws in his counting method, allowing him to continually count out of order. Yet, number sense is central to Bink's learning of key math operations like addition and according to Creative Curriculum and the state standards, Bink should be able to count up to 20. In Bink's portfolio from September 12, 2011-May 3, 2012, there are only five observation notes; indicating that Ms. Jane has not been consistently checking in on Bink's learning and development. Ms. Jane's underestimation of Bink's abilities are concerning given that it is the end of the school year and Bink will enter kindergarten in a few months. Other children from similar backgrounds will have been taught to count in the correct order, so Ms. Jane is putting Bink at a disadvantage by not correcting his error and teaching him the proper way, although she probably does not realize it. However, by not teaching him, Ms. Jane is sending the message to Bink that telling him that he is not capable of counting correctly. Ms. Jane expects Bink to answer in incomplete sentences, get distracted, and need help completing a task, which is exactly what happens when she asks him to come over to the library area to help her retell the book *The Very Hungry Caterpillar*:

Ms. Jane shows Bink the book, *The Very Hungry Caterpillar*: "Do you remember this book?"

Bink: "Caterpillar."

Ms. Jane: "Yes, it's about a very hungry caterpillar."

Bink: "Butterfly."

Ms. Jane: "Yes, you are right; he does turn into a butterfly. Let's see how."

Bink turns to the first page: "Ooh a sun. The sun and the moon. A caterpillar."

Ms. Jane: "It's inside." She turns the page.

Bink: "A caterpillar waked up."

Ms. Jane: "He popped out of the…"

Bink begins turning pages, grabbing several pages in his hand and

turning them to the left.

Ms. Jane: "Bink, do you want to continue with the book?"

He nods: "The caterpillar hungry."

Ms. Jane: "Excellent, he is hungry."

Bink points to the food: "Apple. Plum. Orange."

Ms. Jane asks Bink to count.

Bink turns the page. "Look ice cream. What's that?"

Ms. Jane: "Sausage."

Bink turns the page: "He's feeling better."

Ms. Jane: "Yes, after he ate the leaf. What's happening now?"

Bink: "He's getting bigger and bigger. Gonna turn into a

butterfly." He turns the page: "He's a butterfly" (observation, June 8,

2012).

In the above vignette, Bink is clearly excited about the book. Ms. Jane capitalizes on this

excitement by using leading questions to persuade Bink to retell the story of the *Very Hungry

Caterpillar*. Ms. Jane's attempts to force Bink to follow the exact plot of the book are thwarted

by Bink's urge to flip ahead through the pages. Ms. Jane does not tell Bink that he missed pages;

she allows him to tell the story his way. In a way, this response to Bink is child-centered because

Ms Jane allows Bink to display his book handling skills, but because she does not expect more of

him, like the ability to look through a book, turning page by page, which is an age-appropriate

expectation (New Jersey State Department of Education, 2009), Ms. Jane might be seen as

curtailing Bink's learning. Similarly, in this interaction Ms. Jane does not correct Bink's grammar usage, or ask for full-sentences when Bink chooses to answer with a single word. Bink is an English language learner, who needs opportunities to engage in conversations so he can become more comfortable and proficient in English.

Since Ms. Jane sees Bink as deficient and lacking in focus, she does not view him as capable, even when his performance in the activity shows that he is. Ms. Jane chooses to focus on the activity that she has decided on instead of using the time with Bink to help him improve on counting or conversing; this adherence to her chosen activity can be seen in the following vignette:

Ms. Jane has the game Bugged Out on the table. Bink sits down at the table next to Ms. Jane for his turn.

Ms. Jane: "How are you?"

Bink smiles.

Ms. Jane: "Good. Ready?"

Bink smiles.

Ms. Jane points to the bugs that she has lined up on the table: "Red blue red blue."

Bink: "Red blue red blue." He touches each bug as well.

Ms. Jane: "Now, what do you think comes next?"

Bink: "Red." Bink adds a red bug then a blue bug.

Ms. Jane and Bink: "Red blue red blue red blue" (observation, May 10, 2012).

Bink understood this patterning lesson very quickly, but there was no praise from Ms. Jane. In fact, there were very few words from Ms. Jane at all. It seems odd that when this child, who Ms.

Jane seems to think is struggling, shows promise with a lesson the conversation relates directly to the task at hand with no feedback given about the patterning done by Bink. Since Bink was able to represent a simple pattern, Ms. Jane should have found more ways to challenge Bink. For example, she could have capitalized on his enjoyment of the patterns and used this lesson to work on his counting and conversation. This would have helped Bink realize that what he was doing was correct and allowed him to learn to be proud of his accomplishments.

Although I only observed Ms. Jane's interactions with Bink over four weeks, it appears that her expectations of Bink are limiting the opportunities he has to expand on his learning of academic concepts and skills in small group interactions. Bink is not being taught to use the English language, to handle books properly, or to count in order. There was a lack of observation notes about these three skills in his portfolio. When Bink did understand the concept that Ms. Jane was teaching, she does not expand the lesson to allow Bink to show if he can make different varieties of patterns. Delpit (2006) would say that Ms. Jane is ignoring Bink's patterning fluency in favor of trying to stick to teaching the skill that she had planned because he is a Black student who does not adhere to Ms. Jane's ideals. In these ways, Ms. Jane is holding Bink back from achieving his academic potential. Ms. Jane's lack of confidence in Bink's abilities reflects deficit assumptions. As a low-income, Black, immigrant, English language learner, Ms. Jane underestimates Bink's abilities.

However, during "small group," Ms. Jane offers a lot of encouragement to her students. She smiles and praises the children by telling them exactly what they did correctly. She allows the children to provide incorrect answers and does not chastise them for these answers; instead, she focuses on the positive when that positive is within the expectations that she holds for those students. Ms. Jane does not see beyond the limiting academic expectation she has of each student, however. Since Ms. Jane sees Dora as a bright student who is eager to learn, she does not question why Dora does not speak during one of her interactions, and she also does not assist Dora with the underlying issue of color identification that arises during the patterning lesson. Since Ms. Jane sees Bink as struggling, she places words in his mouth and ignores counting errors, not allowing him to try out his new English skills or expand upon his patterning knowledge. She may see herself as one of her students' people, but her interactions with Dora and Bink suggest that she does not have very high expectations for them.

Developmentally Appropriate, but not Culturally Responsive

When Ms. Jane reflected on what her class thinks of her, she said, "They call me mommy. I think that says it all. A lot of times they hang onto me and say I love you. They love school. They say they love me and I'm their teacher. They say all kinds of nice things" (interview, April 17, 2012). Both students echoed Ms. Jane's perceptions. When asked what he thinks about his teacher, Bink replied, "I like her, so I go to school every day" (interview, May 23, 2012), while Dora said, "Can give me hugs all the time. I like her" (interview, May 23, 2012). Likewise, the students believed that Ms. Jane cared about them. As Dora said, "Loves me" (interview, May 23, 2012) and Bink said, "She like me" (interview, May 23, 2012). In the interviews, Bink and Dora spoke of the same notion of love and family that Ms. Jane brought up in her interviews. This idea of the classroom as a family may come out of Ms. Jane's attempt to insert herself into the children's culture, since she saw herself as having been part of their community when she was young. By focusing so heavily on this idea of the class as a family, Ms. Jane glosses over the differences between herself and her students, even the differences among the students. While she individualizes lessons developmentally and sets her classroom up to look culturally responsive, she does not include individual children's cultural and personal differences.

At first glance, Ms. Jane appears to be a caring and child-centered educator who enacts a curriculum that allows for the give and take between students and teacher. However, upon closer inspection it is evident that all the lessons that are taught to Dora and Bink are derived from themes chosen by Ms. Jane, a white teacher. At the same time, Ms. Jane does not seem to have high academic expectations for her students as she does not scaffold Dora or Bink to learn concepts and behaviors that will prepare them for kindergarten. For each of the small group activities, Ms. Jane did not deviate from her goals regardless of whether Bink or Dora showed that they had mastered the skill or did not understand a concept. In choosing to stay with the lesson as planned despite the differing needs of her students, Ms. Jane was choosing what knowledge was important and whose "cultural capital" deserved to be acknowledged (Delpit, 1995; Copple & Bredekamp, 2009). In doing so, Ms. Jane may be helping to reproduce many of the social stereotypes about black, inner city children like Bink and Dora (Lubeck, 1994). Delpit (2006) has argued that progressive approaches to education such as developmentally appropriate practices reflect a middle-class way of knowing that does not serve the best interests of African American students. Bink and Dora already face challenges because they are Black and poor therefore entering school academically ready according to Delpit is important if these children are to be seen as capable.

Summary

When looking at PreK A and PreK B, I found myself drawn to the child-centered appearance of PreK B. However, beneath the surface the two classrooms were not as different as

I first thought. It is interesting that the surface differences are not necessarily differences in understanding, just in teaching styles.

Cross Case Analysis

When entering into PreK A and PreK B, an observer would notice many differences, but beyond the surface, both Ms. Becky and Ms. Jane shared similar goals. Because of their expectations for their Black students, the way these teachers enacted their academic goals were often not in the best interests of their Black students.

Similar Goals but Different Practices

The literature on teacher expectations shows that teachers make assumptions based on their first impressions about students. Teachers do not wait to see what the students are capable of doing in class before making assumptions about their students' academic abilities (Rosenthal & Jacobsen, 1968; Rist, 1970; and Ladson-Billings, 2009). Often, these expectations are made based on appearance and social class (Rist, 1970; Ladson-Billings, 2009). By creating lessons that provide no challenge or no assistance for students, the teacher is creating an environment that is setting those students up for failure; likewise, expectations that are too high can create the same problem. When a teacher places expectations too high, the teacher can end up doing the work for the student, not letting the student actually learn or achieve; according to Rist (1970), this occurs when the teacher has made up her mind about the competence level of the student, allowing that student no choice but to be a low achiever.

Both Ms. Becky and Ms. Jane's expectations were that the children do the academics that they wanted them to learn, not excel, not do better than, but just get through the basics. According to Delpit (2006) and Lubeck (1985) teaching academic skills is what many teachers think Black children need, as well as what the Black community may want. Lubeck (1985) looked at two preschool classrooms, one middle class and white, the other low-income and

Black; she found that the low-income preschool focused more on teaching academic skills and promoting group growth, as opposed to the individual learning and communication skills focused on in the middle-class and white preschool. These ideas of focusing on skill-based learning and promoting group growth can be seen in Ms. Becky and Ms. Jane's teaching. Both teachers used whole group as a vehicle for promoting their chosen themes through questions of the day and book reading. Likewise, the focus on skill-based learning and promoting group growth could be seen in Ms. Becky and Ms. Jane's small group plans and interactions as every small group was focused on a single academic skill and that activity was taught to every child in the class, despite the children's variety of skill levels.

Ms. Becky was very up front with her focus on academic skills, while Ms. Jane, on the other hand, seemed like she was more about developmentally appropriate teaching. However, in both classrooms the focal children were not being taught the lessons that they needed to succeed in public school because the teachers' academic goals were limited to rote memorization, as evidenced by the repeated morning message and date during whole group. Social knowledge such as asking questions and holding conversations, were not emphasized during small group in either class as the focus of both teachers was on math and literacy skills to the detriment of all other areas of the children's development. The tasks, although focused on specific math or literacy skills, were often meaningless to the students whose skill level was either above or below the lesson. This was very apparent when Ms. Jane tried to teach the Bugged Out pattern lesson to Dora, but Dora could not make the pattern because she did not know the colors. Instead of teaching her the colors, Ms. Jane simply told Dora the answers to ensure that the lesson would be completed. Likewise, when Bink completed the same lesson with ease, Ms. Jane did not use the time to work on other skills he needed improvement on. She simply checked off that the patterning lesson was completed. Ms. Jane taught each child the same skill despite his or her understanding of the concept or skill that was the focus of small group.

Graue (2005) argues that kindergarten and preschool teachers tend to have a prototypical student that they teach to, and these preexisting ideals for students may influence their expectations for their real students. From the observations conducted in both classrooms, it seems that Ms. Becky and Ms. Jane taught to a prototypical child rather than individualizing the curriculum to the learning needs of their Black students. For Ms. Becky, her ideal student was one who could sit still and quietly for long periods of time. She praised the child who accomplished that: Princess, while admonishing the child who failed, Diego. During whole group, Ms. Becky expected Diego to be disruptive and put him in situations that made it very difficult for him to behave in accordance with her view of acceptable behavior: sitting quietly and still for at least fifteen minutes. Ms. Jane stated that her goal for her students was for them, "to grow on their terms" (interview, April 17, 2012). She took this view as license to allow her students to maintain lower performances than the state standards suggest they should be doing. Ms. Jane minimized the flaws in Dora and Bink's performances in small group when they did not get the correct answers and led them through the activities without really teaching them the concepts behind the lessons. As a result of their lower expectations, neither Ms. Jane nor Ms. Becky individualized their interactions with the focal students and overlooked many opportunities to work with their students on the skills they needed to enhance.

When observing the teaching of Black students, Ladson-Billings (2009) found that White teachers do not always have expectations that allow their students to be successful. While it could be argued that Ms. Becky and Ms. Jane's focus on academics teaches the skills that Black students need to be successful in school (Delpit, 2006; Lubeck 1985), their lowered expectations of the focal students and what they are capable of meant that both teachers failed to support the learning of their students in meaningful ways.

White Teacher Power and Privilege

White privilege is the unseen, invisible force that is an unconscious habit for many White teachers (Sullivan, 2006), like Ms. Becky and Ms. Jane. Because of their positioning, White teachers often have little understanding of how what they teach and how they teach it, privileges certain ways of knowing over others. By controlling the discourse of the classroom, the teacher can push White language and norms on the students, making those who do not typically subscribe to this discourse an outsider (Hallum, 2006). Given their White privilege as teachers, Ms. Becky and Ms. Jane take for granted that choosing the topics for the lessons, creating the social norms of the classroom, and deciding the schedule and duration of events is an exercise of power.

In both PreK A and PreK B, knowledge and classroom discourse for the most part was controlled by the teachers. In this way, the teachers are enacting power over the students, telling them that the teachers' ideas are more important than the students' ideas. For example, both classes were learning about insects and plants, topics chosen by the teachers. As Delpit (2006) would say, Ms. Becky and Ms. Jane are silencing the children's dialogue. They offer only the repetition and reproduction of what they think that Black children need without thought to culturally responsive teaching (Ladson Billings, 2009).

Culturally responsive teaching means that teachers recognize and respond to the learning differences of students; a teacher using culturally responsive teaching creates an atmosphere that provides students from different backgrounds with a safe environment to express their pride in their backgrounds as well as their goals for success in the present and the future. For White teachers, culturally responsive teaching means that they must recognize that there are multiple perspectives with which to view the world, opening their eyes to their own White privilege and being open to see new ways of constructing knowledge (Villegas & Lucas, 2002). By being open to new ideas, new ways of learning and by building connections between the students' lives and the work they are doing in school, culturally responsive teachers support Black students to become accomplished with the discourses of schooling.

Culturally responsive teaching is not fully realized in PreK A and PreK B. Ms. Becky is oblivious to the use of culturally responsive teaching because she does not acknowledge the diverse backgrounds of her students in her classroom environment or lesson plans and does not state in any of her interviews or lesson plans that she is working to create educational change for her students or understand how her students construct knowledge. One example of her lack of understanding of the students' backgrounds is when she taught about Father's Day even though most of the children were being raised by single mothers. Ms. Jane, on the other hand, seems to try to use some elements of culturally responsive teaching; her classroom is set up to give the children a feeling of acceptance: the flags from their countries of heritage on the wall, the native costumes in dramatic play, and the multicultural books around the room. She also tries to set up her whole group time as a community of learners in which the class acts as a community, even though she chooses the topic and questions. However, her efforts at culturally responsive teaching fall apart during small group, which is completely teacher directed and without individualization.

While it has been argued by scholars that African American children need to know how to navigate and use the academic discourse of school, the academics that Ms. Becky and Ms.

Jane are focusing on in their small and large groups do not seem to be working in the best interests of the focal students because the teachers' White privilege seems to be influencing their expectations. Ms. Becky and Ms. Jane have not become socio-culturally conscious enough to see beyond their own point of view, nor have they started to try to understand how their students construct knowledge, so the lessons are all presented in the same manner. Neither teacher is really getting the children to the levels of literacy and numeracy that they need to be at to be successful in kindergarten, and both seem to be underestimating their students' abilities.

While the focal students try to show their teachers that they have more to offer, Ms. Becky and Ms. Jane tend to overlook these offers in favor with sticking to their scripts. Since Ms. Becky and Ms. Jane are not promoting their students' individual ways of constructing knowledge or using their own information about their students' lives to design the lessons, neither teacher is realizing how using culturally responsive teaching could help them prepare their students to be successful in kindergarten and raise their expectations of their students. For example, Diego makes personal connections to the literacy lessons, pointing out when reading a book with Ms. Becky reminds him of a book at home; but since his offerings do not fit into Ms. Becky's expectations, she does not pick up on them. Similarly, Ms. Jane ignores Bink's offers of his patterning skills as proof to Ms. Jane that he is more than just a low-achiever, but instead of picking up on Bink's offer, Ms. Jane continues to maintain her viewpoint. Likewise, since Ms. Jane says she thinks Dora is a bright child, she leads Dora through lessons instead of picking up on the silence that Dora offers as proof that something else may be happening with the child. By overlooking the knowledge and understandings offered up by their focal students, Ms. Becky and Ms. Jane favor a scripted curriculum aimed at a prototypical preschooler devoid of race and class instead of embracing the promise of their Black students.

Conclusion

In conclusion, preschool teachers hold expectations of their students and these expectations are expressed by teachers in a myriad of ways from the way they set up classroom environments to the instructional events they enact on a daily basis. White preschool teachers may see themselves as part of the Black community in which they teach, but it does not change the fact that they are still White, and therefore have a certain privilege in public schooling. If teachers become aware of how crucial their expectations and interactions are for the futures of their students, perhaps they will shun the forced hand raising and quiet sitting that has become so ingrained in White American education and instead listen to their Black students to create curricula and classrooms where student knowledge and ways of being are truly privileged. It is very sad to think of a world in which a four-year-old has resigned to being hated by teachers and thinking he will never be good at school. As educators, it is our job to show every student that he or she can succeed.

References

Barnett, W.S., Epstein, D.J., Carolan, M.E., Fitzgerald, J., Ackerman, D.J., & Friedman, A.H. (2010). The state of preschool 2010. Retrieved October 26, 2011, from http://nieer.org/yearbook/

Barnett, W.S., Carolan, M.E., Fitzgerald, J., & Squires, J.H. (2012). *The state of preschool 2012: State preschool yearbook*. New Brunswick, NJ: National Institute for Early Education Research.

Bredecamp, S. & Copple, C. (Eds.) (1997). *Developmentally appropriate practice in Early Childhood programs*. Washington, DC: National Association for Educators of Young Children.

Cazden, C. B. (2001). *Classroom discourse: The language of teaching and learning*. Portsmouth, NH: Heinemann.

Copple, C. & Bredekamp, S. (2009). *Developmentally appropriate practice in early childhood programs* (3rd ed.). Washington, DC: NAEYC.

Delpit, L. (2006). *Other people's children*. New York: The New Press.

Dewey, J. (2011). *The child and the curriculum*. Chicago: The University of Chicago Press.

Dewey, J. (1997). *Education and experience*. New York: Free press.

Dodge, D. T., Heroman, C., Colker, L. J., Bickart, T. S. (2012). *The Creative Curriculum*. (Vol. 1). Washington, D.C.: Teaching Strategies.

Education Law Center, 2011, *The history of Abbott v. Burke*. Retrieved August 11, 2011, from http://www.edlawcenter.org/cases/abbott-v-burke/abbott-history.html

Elias, M. J., Zins, J. E., Weissberg, R. P., Frey, K. S., Greenberg, M. T., Haynes, N. M., Kessler, R., Schwab-Stone, M. E., & Shriver, T. P. (1997). *Promoting social and emotional learning: Guidelines for educators*. Alexandria, VA: ASCD.

Etheridge, E. A. & King, J. R. (2005). Calendar math in preschool and primary classrooms: Questioning the curriculum. *Early Childhood Education Journal* 32 (5): (291-296).

Faubion, J.D. (Ed.). (1994). *Michael Foucault - power*. New York: The New Press.

Frede, E.C. & Barnett, W. S. (2007). Who goes to preschool and why does it matter?. *Preschool Policy Brief* 15: 1-15.

Frede, E. C., Jung, K., Barnett, W. S., & Figueras, A. (2009). The APPLES blossom: Abbott Preschool Program Longitudinal Effects Study (APPLES) preliminary results through 2nd grade.

Gestwicki, C. (2011). *Developmentally appropriate practice* (4th ed.). Belmont, CA: Wadsworth.

Graue, M. E. (2005). (De)centering the kindergarten prototype in the child-centered classroom. In Ryan, S. & Grieshaber, S. (Eds.) *Practical Transformations and transformational practices: Globalization, postmodernism, and early childhood education.* (p. 39-59). New York: Elsevier.

Hallam, P. J. (2006). "Crossing cultural borders through authentic assessment of classroom discourse: A Freirean Approach." In Lee, V. & Helfand, J. (Eds). *Identifying race and transforming whiteness in the classroom.* (p. 47-67). New York: Peter Lang.

Lown, J. (2002). Circle time: The perceptions of teachers and pupils. Educational Psychology in Practice 18 (2): 93-103.

Lubeck, S. (1985). *Sandbox society*. Philadelphia: The Falmer Press.

Lubeck, S. (1994). The politics of developmentally appropriate practice. In Mallory, B. L. & New, R. S. (Eds.). Diversity & developmentally appropriate practices (p. 17-44). New York: Teachers College Press.

New Jersey State Department of Education. (2009). *New Jersey preschool teaching and learning standards of quality*. Retrieved November 4, 2013 from http://www.state.nj.us/education/cccs/preschool.htm

Rist, R. C. (1970). Student social class and teacher expectations: The self-fulfilling prophecies in ghetto education. *Harvard Educational Review* 70(3), 257-265.

Rosenthal, R. & Jacobson, L. (1968). *Pygmalion in the classroom.* New York: Holt, Rinehart, and Winston, Inc.

Sansone, A. (2017). Preschool Teacher-Student Interactions and Expectations. Saarbrücken, Germany: LAP Lambert.

Sullivan, S. (2006). *Revealing whiteness*. Indianapolis, IN: Indiana University Press.

Villegas, A. M. & Lucas, T. (2002). Preparing culturally responsive teachers: Rethinking the curriculum. Journal of Teacher Education 53 (1), 20-32.

Williams, L. R. (1999). "Determining the early childhood curriculum: The evolution of goals and strategies through consonance and controversy." In Seefeldt, C. (Ed.) *The early childhood curriculum: Current findings in theory and practice* (3rd ed.). (p. 1-27). New York: Teachers College Press.